National Preservation

or

National Perversion ...LGBT

What Legacy Will We Leave?

by
Tim Chipps

Also by Tim Chipps

Make America Right Again

Ominous Alliance

Gross Injustice

Citizens Handbook

Follyhood

Published and distributed by
Artisan Vintage Works

Printed in the United States of America

To contact us or to order our publications
please visit our website:
artisanvintageworks.com

Index

Chapter 1

A Heritage Worthy of Preservation

America, the beautiful.
America, the home of the brave.

Oh, beautiful, for spacious skies, for amber waves of grain, for purple mountains majesty, above the fruited plains. America, America, God shed his grace on thee...or will he shed tears?

It's true, we really have been blessed by God. What an honor and a privilege to have been born free in America! "One nation under God" is our motto and "In God we trust" is printed on our currency. And though we don't always agree on everything, America still remains the freest and most prosperous nation in the world. From the Statue of Liberty in New York to the Liberty Bell in Philadelphia, these monuments are markers of freedom, placed in remembrance of those who sacrificed even their lives so that we can be free. From the Washington Monument to the Lincoln Memorial in Washington D.C. Remember the Tomb of the Unknown Soldier in Arlington, Virginia? These are markers in time, signifying the struggles and hardships wrought by brave men and women of noble character, exemplifying courage, dignity, honor and sacrifice made by many average ordinary citizens in our nation's past. To most of us these virtuous men and women are heroes, cherished throughout our history. We have a lot to be thankful for and we understand this privilege and our obligation to live up to a standard, worthy of those who sacrificed so much on our behalf.

I remember as a child being asked by my mother, "What are you going to be when you grow up?" The answer always changed, the older I became. I thought I would be a policeman or fireman, maybe a pilot or pro football player. There was always a brave hero or gallant role model who exemplified a person to look up to. John Wayne, the famous cowboy of the west, always portrayed a stout and good man, ready to stand up for the truth and do what was right.

From the early pioneers who landed at Plymouth Rock in 1620, sailing on the Mayflower ship from England, searching for a land where they could have religious freedom and an opportunity to provide a good living for their family, acquire land and homestead, the stories in our nation's history are countless. They vouch to confirm and attest to the courage and willingness of Americans to work hard and remain steadfast in their determination to establish a country of their own, one free from the rulers, monarchs and tyrants they left behind. This was no easy task and though many hardships would be encountered, by the grace of God and divine providence, they would advance and achieve their goal, whatever the cost might be. This is the story of America.

It is our heritage and our history, and though it only dates back formally to 1776, it really started in the early 1600s. What is so fascinating and remarkable is the long list of accomplishments that have been made or attained in this short period of time, less than 400 years. Most cultures in society worldwide are descriptive of nations that date back 5,000 years or more. China, Russia, Europe and Africa have histories of this nature. Some empires such as Rome, who ruled the earth for over 1,000 years, have risen and fallen. These are history lessons of actual events occurring for all to see and learn from. We must be aware of the entrapments that cause the fall of very great and powerful nations in order to ensure our future posterity and avoid the pitfalls that contributed to the collapse of many prior strong and mighty nations.

Our Declaration of Independence is based upon the relevance of our dependence upon God, our creator. The first amendment of the constitution was written as a guarantee of religious freedom and the exercise thereof. Did you know that there are over 320,000 church buildings in America? The population of the United States is presently approximately 326 million. Of that total, over 73 percent are of Judeo-Christian and biblical faiths. The only real doctrinal differences occur amongst denominations that cite scripture interpretation as a reason or purpose for method of worship or doctrinal discrepancies. By and large though, the gospels depicting Jesus' life, death and resurrection with the epistles (letters to the churches written by the apostles of Jesus Christ) are central in the message of salvation to all believers.

The Bible has been the chief instrument for establishing the standards by which we live, not just in our personal lives, but also within our society as a whole. And much of law, including the Constitution and Bill of Rights, is derived from this great volume of his-story written in the greatest compilation of history known to mankind. That is what the word "noel" means—good news! The important reason for distinguishing these facts is to ultimately give proper credit to the one responsible for the hope and encouraging faith we experience as the benefactors of God's goodness, faithfulness and long-suffering patience. The scripture says it best: Eph.3:15 "From whom every family in heaven and on earth derives its name"–thanks be to God for his kingdom, glory and power–forever. Amen.

The simple truth is, we have much to be thankful for. Since the invention of the gas engine and our discovery of how to harness electricity in the mid-1800s, we have been able to advance in technology and science at an extremely rapid rate. We have invented and discovered many interesting necessities, much of which we take for granted. Discovering cures for many diseases and discovering galaxies in deep space, even landing on the moon, all this has taken place just over the past 165 years. There's no telling how far we will go in advancements and profitable discoveries.

The one stable and consistent factor in all of these marvelous achievements is the fact that God remains the same, an ever-present help in our time of need. He is not like the shifting shadows that move with the differing times of day. He is the solid rock and anchor of humanity, the creator of heaven and earth, the father of his multitude of children who gather and congregate to acknowledge and thank him for his many blessings and the protection and peace he has extended to us, as his people.

This is what made our country great and truly, we must preserve this national distinction in order to pass on to future generations of Americans our key to success and assurance of posterity. This heritage of America's values has its origins in our faith and reliance upon almighty God, and only in this notion of understanding will we be able to overcome the obstacles and evermore complicated issues we will be facing as time expires into the future.

In that respect, I am a conservative. This is

one area we must preserve and cherish–what our ancestors passed on to us, knowing and often warning us of the consequences of neglect and the potential result of such action. For those who do not yet understand the implications of such neglect, we need only remind them of the clear and undeniable providence of almighty God during the 12 wars America engaged in, and the peace and prosperity we enjoy as a privilege. If we abuse this trust and choose to become "mockers of God," ignoring his requirements and turning a deaf ear to his many warnings to us, both in word and by example. Remember, "Do not be deceived, God is not mocked, whatever a person sows, that he also shall reap." (Gal 6:7).

There are many who will dismiss this as Doom's Day language and someday very soon they will discover the fallacy and foolishness of their presumption. For those of us who know better, I wish to say thank you for showing an earnest respect for our country's rich history. I also must alert you to the extremely graphic nature of discourse in the discussion and dialogue that will be revealed in the coming chapters of this book. It is with regret that we are forced to enter into the new age, bold and lawless acquiescence of behavior advocated by extreme liberal, atheist and secular-humanist sects within our society, but to ignore these fraction elements and to allow a continuum without staunch protest will assure the inevitable and absolute collapse of the American culture. It will be hard for some even to believe what has and is transpiring right in front of our eyes.

Chapter 2
Throwing Off All Restraints

Many of us have witnessed the tumultuous political movement and clarion call for change during the 2016 presidential campaign. Let's face it, American citizens have had enough of the far-left radical liberal bureaucrats and their "out of touch" policies. People are demanding "real change" in many areas affecting their everyday lives. The "earmarks" of Obama's eight-year term include: The most stagnant economy in U.S. history since the Great Depression in 1933; his "no-borders" strategy dealing with illegal immigrants and mass importation of over 680 thousand Muslim/Islamic refugees from the middle east and their potential terror threat; his overwhelming government regulations and higher tax rates; his special-interest groups such as the LGBT "same-sex marriage" initiative; his promotion and U.S. taxpayer funding of abortion, expanded to sponsor worldwide organizations abroad. Did you know that over 60 million abortions have been performed in the U.S.A. to date?

Through the illicit subversive act of appointing 329 federal judges to the U.S. courts in order to accomplish his special-interest agenda, he then used these surrogate judges who insidiously usurped the authority of both houses of Congress to get "law/ precedent established" by circumventing the legal process and bypassing lawmakers. He appointed an additional 250 LGBT (lesbian, gay, bisexual and transgender) individuals to executive cabinet positions, ensuring the success of his plans. He, through the NEA (National Education Association), has mandated this LGBT curricula be taught to all children from K through 12th grades, to accept, adapt and embrace this immoral practice which consists of less than 4 percent of our nation's populations. (Please note: This is all on public record and I welcome you to fact-check).

The son of Barack Hussein Obama Sr., a Kenyan-African Muslim/Islamic, stated Obama has embraced these extremely radical views his entire life. In his term as U.S. Senator he stated that "the U.S. Constitution is a flawed document from which we must break free." He is on record as the most liberal senator to ever be elected. During his eight-year term in the White House he gave away 33 billion U.S. taxpayer dollars to the nation of Iran (this is the #1 terrorist-sponsored nation known worldwide). Mr. Obama has incurred more U.S. debt, totaling 19.7 trillion U.S. taxpayer dollars, during his eight-year term (please note: this is more debt than all previous administrations combined). In other words, all 43 presidents prior to Obama combined did not incur this much debt. It's unprecedented in U.S. history.

These are only a few of his accomplishments while in the White House. It would take hundreds of pages to chronicle this man's actions and deeds while occupying the highest seat in our land. He will truly be written down in history as "the man of lawlessness." That is his legacy. The real question now is: will our elected officials "stand up" against this onslaught of deviant and degenerate policy establishment? Or will they "cow-down" to the intimidation of the 4 percent/few in the radical fringe minority which advocates these demented actions of licentiousness? Where are the noble men and women of America? If nothing is done to reverse this trend of ineptitude, America's days will be numbered (as described in the Book of Daniel 5:25-28) and we will soon see the "handwriting on the wall." Time is running out folks!

The following are quotes from Barack Hussein Obama, statements he has made publicly concerning the issues and agenda he sought to pass as a U.S. Senator from early 2006 through both his terms as President through 2016.

Quote: "Whatever we once were, we are no longer a Christian nation—at least not just. We are also a Jewish nation, a Muslim nation, a Buddhist nation, and a Hindu nation, and a nation of non-believers."

Quote: "I believe in evolution, scientific inquiry and global warming. I believe in free speech, whether politically correct or politically incorrect, and I am suspicious of using government to impose anybody's religious beliefs—including my own on non-believers."

Quote: "At some fundamental level religion does not allow for compromise. It insists on the impossible. If God has spoken, then followers are expected to live up to God's edicts, regardless of the consequences. To base one's own life on such uncompromising commitments may be sublime; to base our policy on such commitments would be a dangerous thing."

Quote: "Our journey is not complete until our gay brothers and sisters are treated like anyone else under the law, for if we are truly created equal, then surely the love we commit to one another must be equal as well."

This is what Barack Obama believes by "breaking free" from all restraints in our society. He states: "Churches won't work with you, though, just out of the goodness of their hearts. They'll talk a good game on sermon Sunday maybe, or a special offering for the homeless, but if push comes to shove, they won't really move unless you can show them how it will help them pay their heating bill." He said in his book: "I found God in myself and I loved her, I loved her fiercely–lights."

Evidently Mr. Obama struggled immensely with gender identify himself. I am not certain, but it appears as if psychosis could be the explanation. He goes on to say: "In the Catholic school, when it came time to pray, I would pretend to close my eyes, then peek around the room. Nothing happened, no angels descended."

He states: "Once I found an issue enough people cared about, I could take them into action. With enough actions I could start to build power. Issues, action, power, self-interest, I liked these concepts. They bespoke a certain hard-headedness, a worldly lack of sentiment (politics, not religion)."

He was quite drawn to the idea of exerting power regarding his self-interest in government.

"For in the end, laws are just words on a page– words that are sometimes malleable, opaque, as dependent on context and trust as they are in a story or a poem or a promise to someone, words, whose meanings are subject to erosion, sometimes collapsing in the blink of an eye."

So law, or the constitution of many laws, to Mr. Obama are just words on a page, collapsing in the blink of an eye. This man was elected President of the United States!

The above quotes from Barack Obama should give you some idea of the character he displays, or rather the lack thereof. Truly, these are the words of a spiritual degenerate who, in Biblical terms, is referred to as a reprobate.

Barack Obama clearly understood that he could not go through the legal process of legitimately passing a law through both houses of Congress to legalize and pass his "gay marriage" agenda. Our lawmakers would never pass it, so he intentionally subverted due process of law in order to circumvent (bypass) the lawmakers and use the federal judges as surrogates in order to establish his policy. He appointed and installed these radical LGBT (lesbian, gay, bisexual, transgender) judges as "lifetime" judges for this very purpose, knowing that few persons with presumptive "super-legislative power" could get it done.

This "loophole" in our system of lawmaking must be either reversed or closed. It has posed a false tenant and wrongfully established a false precedent for laws to be established that would never otherwise have a chance. This illegal process used by Obama to appoint judges with radical views to get laws established through super-legislative presumption must be "stopped dead in its tracks."

If Congress refuses to impeach these justices for "breach of trust," it appears that a "constitutional amendment" to limit justices of this kind of power is the remedy to this dangerous pattern of subversion of law. I believe decisions of this magnitude should be required to visit and be submitted to both houses of Congress for review, redress and debate before any precedent is established. This issue is of paramount concern and is vitally in need of conclusive resolve. This country's future is at stake, and our constitution requires it, as does any hope for the future.

Chapter 3

Where are the Men and Women of Noble Character?

Just to be sure we are on the same page, we must define correctly the term "noble character." There are two definitions according to the English translation. One implies the notable birth of a person pertaining to class or rank, being of royal blood. The other definition is quite different and implies that a person of high moral standards, honesty, integrity, uprightness and virtue, are character qualities that person has acquired or attained.

This is the "noble character" I am referring to. In the Bible there are many references to the word noble. Isaiah 32:8 reads: "The nobleman devises noble plans and by noble plans he stands." Paul the Apostle tells us: "Whatever is true, whatever is noble, whatever is lovely, whatever is excellent, whatever is praiseworthy: think about such things." (Philippians 4:8 NIV)

And again Solomon states in Proverbs 8:6: "Listen, for I will speak noble things; and the opening of my lips will reveal right things." The mental and moral qualities of a person define his or her character. Noble character is developed in a person over time through learning and experience. It requires a dedication to doing the right thing and making wise choices. Truly it requires self-discipline. God spoke of Solomon, author of proverbs, as the wisest man to ever live.

The aspiration to attaining "noble character" is very important, especially in the sight of God. Why then, in this day and age that we live in, is "noble character" so rare to see in many people we associate with?

It is very apparent that this quality in a person's character is becoming harder to find in people today. So rare, it is almost as if this characteristic has diminished within modern society. There are many reasons for this decline. Most children are not taught this attribute or quality characteristic in public schools due to the debased curricula being taught in the schools. The basic standards of right and wrong have been replaced with "preference in choice" for students. In other words, if you want to do it, that's okay, and if you don't want to do it, that's okay too! This baseless form of teaching places little emphasis on any standards at all, undermining the very foundation of education and rendering valueless much of the instruction children are receiving.

As President Theodore Roosevelt stated: "To educate a man in mind and not morals is to educate a menace to society." And as C.S. Lewis stated: "Education without values is as useful as it seems rather to make man a more clever devil." And as G.K. Chesterton said: "Education is simply the 'soul of a society' as it passes from one generation to another."

So what is the "soul of a society" if it becomes totally void of "noble character?" All we need do is look around, it's everywhere you turn. What has happened to us here in America? The NEA (National Education Association) has embraced the LGBT (lesbian, gay, bi-sexual, transgender) agenda. This union–as it refers itself to–has created curricula, teaching grades K-12 concerning "gender identity." Rather than being considered noble, virtuous, honest or having integrity, there are a new set of character qualities being taught, inculcating the base, coarse, immoral, deceitful, tolerant and rude. Do these terms better represent the character qualities seemingly so prevalent in our society today? Do you think it is possible that we have neglected to teach our youth the basic foundational principles, morals and values so critically important in their development in order to become responsible adults capable of functioning in a positive manner of conduct?

The American public school system has failed miserably at the task of education. It is not the fault of dedicated teachers. There are many, many, very dedicated teachers in our public school system who hold to a high standard of virtue. The parents are the primary decision-makers overseeing the education of their children. They must be aware of the influences that saturate their children's minds on a daily basis. The NEA has adopted this policy, embracing the LGBT (sexually deviant) open agenda, teaching American students that this deviant lifestyle is not only acceptable, but in many cases inevitable. We were shocked when we found out several years ago that fourth-grade students were being instructed and taught how to put condoms on bananas.

This, my friend, goes far beyond that level. In this "new age" of "bold liberalism," tolerance of any unnatural behavior is now acceptable. The laws protecting citizens from vile perversion are now being challenged and in some cases already being changed in order to accommodate/protect the LGBT (or sexually deviant). Are we voluntarily going to go the way of Sodom and embrace the culture of Gomorrah, knowing the consequences of this decision? (Genesis - 19).

Chapter 4

How Far Down the Abyss Will We Go?

For the global warming community, please note the following scripture: "Above all you must understand that in the last days scoffers will come, scoffing and following their own evil desires. They will say, 'Where is this coming he promised?' Ever since our ancestors died, everything goes on as it has since the beginning of creation. But they deliberately forgot that long ago. By God's word the heavens came into being and the earth was formed out of water and by water. By these waters also the world of that time was deluged and destroyed. By the same word these present heavens and earth are reserved for fire, being kept for the day of judgment and destruction of the ungodly." (2 Peter 3:3-7).

The earth will be 7 times hotter (Rev. 16). Wow, that is really heavy. I don't want to be on the receiving side of that. I can promise you one thing that is absolutely certain: God's word never fails" (Luke 1:37) (Joshua 21:45) (Matthew 24:35).

Do you know that since 1970 over 60 million unborn children have been slaughtered through abortion? Planned Parenthood sells these infants' body parts as an industry (look it up on Google!). How long can we go on and how far do you think we will go before we cross the line of no return? All this foolishness can be stopped by the stroke of a pen. Did you know that?

Chapter 5

The Noble Judges—Dissent

I want to be very clear on the subject of LGBT. I understand and respect the rights of adult individuals who choose to engage in any lifestyle they see fit … as long as they do not violate the rights of others in the process, or harm anyone. I wish it were that simple. The real issue here is not "us versus them" in respecting one another's right to privacy. No, no, this goes much deeper.

For the LGBT community, they not only wish to exercise the right to be immoral, they wish to force and mandate this immorality on 325 million Americans who adamantly disagree and disapprove of that lifestyle. They already introduced their transgender and gay curricula in the national public school system through radical liberal operatives installed at the National Education Association/Union (this is on public record). They also want special treatment using national taxpayer dollars, accommodating alternative rest rooms and "preferred status" as minorities. The list goes on and on.

They desire and intend to get national support, even worldwide support, for their agenda. As the Chief Supreme Court Justice and three associate justices stated in their dissent on the "gay marriage" lawsuit (Obergefell V. Hodges in 2015), listen to what the noble and virtuous Chief Justice John Roberts had to say from the Supreme Court bench at that time: "The majority today relies on its own understanding of what freedom is and must become." He said to the court: "And the deepest problem with the decision was the disrespect it shows the democratic process.

With this decision proponents of same-sex marriage lost the opportunity to win acceptance through the democratic process," he said, "and they lose this just when the winds of change were freshening at their backs." "Five lawyers," he said, "deemed themselves chosen to burst the bonds of history." He further stated that the majority's approach was "deeply disheartening."

The principled and honorable Associate Justice Clarence Thomas said in his dissent that the court "short-circuited" the political process by not allowing states to define marriage for themselves, and he predicts the majority's decision could have "potentially ruinous consequences for religious liberty."

The honorable Associate Justice Antonin Scalia in his dissent called the opinion "judicial Putsch" (or coup). Quote: "The stuff contained in today's opinion has to diminish this court's reputation for clear thinking and sober analysis."

The notable Justice Samuel Alito in his dissent warned that "the court was exceeding the limits of its power," stating: "Americans … should worry about what the majority's claim of power portends." He further stated, "For millennia, marriage was inextricably linked to the one thing that only an opposite-sex couple can do: procreate."

These findings by the noble justices in their dissent actually go on and are quite lengthy. Some other very important points these justices make are as follows:

In his dissent, Chief Justice John G. Roberts Jr. states: "As a result, the court invalidates the marriage laws of more than half the states and orders the transformation of a social institution

that has formed the basis of human society for millennia, for the Kalahari Bushmen and Han Chinese, the Carthaginians, and Aztecs." "Just who do we think we are?"

Justice Antonin Scalia said in his dissent: "The justices in the majority have usurped the power of the people to govern themselves. This is a naked judicial claim to legislative–indeed super-legislative power, a claim fundamentally at odds with our system of government." And finally, stated: "A system of government that makes the people subordinate to a committee of nine elected lawyers does not deserve to be called a democracy."

The noble Justice Clarence Thomas "finds no grounds for a constitutional right to same-sex marriage and says that the majority misconstrues even the concept of freedom." He further states: "Today's decision cast truth aside in its haste to reach a desired result" and "distorts the principles on which this nation was founded. Its decision will have inestimable consequences for our constitution and our society."

Chapter 6

Will God Accept this Behavior?

When a civilized nation, especially one in which the foundation is built upon Biblical principles and the values of Christian virtue, corrupts itself into a state of deviant and degenerate practices of behavior, then approves through government sanction acts of gross immorality, that nation has truly fallen from its former grace.

The dangers inherent by succumbing to this inordinate embracement of vile conduct within our society will inevitably lead to the opening of Pandora's Box as our orthodoxy and creed as Americans diminishes into an abyss of lawless and limitless wrongdoing. There will no longer be any standard by which we should live our lives, no restraints, no restrictions, no limits, no right or wrong, no good or evil. No law at all! It will truly become the precipice for humanity to stand at the edge of, awaiting the great fall of mankind when we ultimately stumble into a pit of total and absolute pandemonium. This will be the direct result of our unconstrained affections and perversion.

This is not what most of us envision for America. Unfortunately, the process of this cycle is clearly in motion and moving forward at an extremely rapid rate. If we the citizens do not stand in firm opposition to this already fast-moving agenda driven by extreme radical left operatives, the establishment of the immoral, unethical and nefarious movement will solidify and become a part of American society. If you believe this is another Doom's Day report predicting America's demise ... think again!

The National Education Association (NEA) has introduced curricula in the public school system mandating teachers to instruct K-12 grades pertaining to "gender identity" where American children can choose for themselves whatever they desire to be, male or female gender, or choose to become something else unknown (other than the gender they are biologically). This is encouraged and offered as an option to the students. Yes, I just said that.

This took place within weeks of the decision in the Supreme Court to establish a precedent for gay marriage to become acceptable in America in 2015. It's outrageous and defies any rational discourse. The special interest judges, appointed by the Clinton and Obama administrations, have yet to be impeached for their breach of trust in their actions leading to this ruling. Both houses of Congress have legitimate authority and power to begin an inquiry into the impeachment process of these few rogue justices. We must notify our lawmakers of our position on this issue and urge them to remove these radical (LGBT Obama) appointees and reverse the cycle of degeneracy and illegitimate practice of attempting to legislate immorality from the benches of the Supreme Court which have no rightful constitutional authority to grant approval for this unlawful action and intrusion upon America's conscience and values.

Chapter 7
What Does God Say About This?

It's important and vital to understand the true meaning of the term "perversion." Its literal definition is "the alteration of something from its original course, meaning or state to a distortion of corruption of what was first intended." "All great evil is the perversion of a good." Although this is a rather unpleasant subject or topic of discourse, it is necessary to understand in order to fully comprehend the depth of depravity that exists in describing the nature of same-sex marriage, homosexuality, and transgender behavior. What's ironic about the leaders of this movement is they have chosen the rainbow as their motto or symbol. The rainbow originally was a sign from God, displayed in the sky to Noah, the Bible patriarch, who was the survivor of the great flood which deluged the entire earth for 40 days and nights because God destroyed mankind at that time, due to the perversion in his heart and desire to do evil (Genesis).

Peter in his second epistle states: "By water also the world of that time was deluged and destroyed. By the same word the present heavens and earth are reserved for fire, being kept for the day of judgment and destruction of ungodly men."

Our present laws pertaining to perversion were derived from these ancient scriptures in the Bible dating back over 5,000 years. The word sodomy, which is a serious crime/felony, came from the city of Sodom in the story of Sodom and Gomorrah found in the Book of Genesis (18-19). Paul the Apostle wrote to the church in Rome warning them, stating:

"Therefore God gave them over in the sinful desires of their hearts to sexual impurity for the degrading of their bodies with one another. They exchanged the truth about God for a lie and worshiped and served created things rather than the creator–who is forever praised. Amen."

"Because of this, God gave them over to shameful lust. Even their women exchanged natural sexual relations for unnatural ones. In the same way the men abandoned natural relations with women and were inflamed with lust for one another. Men committed shameful acts with other men and received in themselves the due penalty for their error." (Romans 1:24-27)

"In a similar way, Sodom and Gomorrah and the surrounding towns gave themselves up to sexual immorality and perversion. They serve as an example of those who suffer the punishment of eternal fire." (Jude 7).

What is really hard to believe, and I find inexplicable, is the brazen defiance illustrated by the LGBT community who has chosen to disregard and ignore the holy scriptures and entire nations historically that participated in these very same actions, events that are well-documented and all result in the same outcome, a true sign of the fact that they have been truly given over to this disparaging condition they choose to embrace.

Chapter 8
Who are the Haters?

Remember during 2007 when President George W. Bush defined marriage for Americans nationally and called for a constitutional amendment protecting this sacred union between "one man and one woman?" "The Defense of Marriage Act" proposed by President Bush passed the House of Representatives by a vote of 342 to 67, and in the Senate by a vote of 85 to 14. These congressional votes and the passage of similar defense marriage laws in 38 states express an overwhelming consensus in our country for protecting the institution of marriage. The numbers speak loudly for themselves.

In the Bible, God refers to marriage as a sacred and holy union. He compares his people to a bride and himself as the bridegroom. This dates back in verifiable script for well over 5,000 years. To profane the act of marriage, an institution created and blessed by God, will be a grotesque attempt to pervert the most precious of unions ordained by our creator to perpetuate humanity in its course, as natural relations of procreation would cease and men will violate the covenant of relationship established by God himself– between both men and women with the creator of the universe. This will be an abomination of the worst kind. We all know in our hearts without a doubt that this is wrong. The judgment rendered in this issue has been made from the beginning of time. Truly, it is likened to playing with fire. Those who chose to play, will inevitably get burned.

In Romans (12:9) Paul states: "Love must be sincere. Hate what is evil, cling to what is good." The advocates of disobedience to God's word, his law and requirements, tell us just the opposite, stating: Love must be insincere, love what is evil and hate what is good. According to the standards of God, which distinguish good from evil, we accept this very basic concept. The proponents of vile perversion, both men and women, have established their own standard (which in reality means there are no standards of right and wrong within this faction).

So who are truly the haters? We who choose to believe God's word and obey it? Or the obstinate and disobedient, immoral crowd who choose to live anyway they see fit? Where do you draw a line for what is acceptable and what is unacceptable? Even hippies know that the laws of nature do not follow this trend of homosexuality. It contradicts all universal laws and properties known to mankind! Philosophically it is abhorrent, scientifically it is impossible, and biologically it is virtually nonexistent in any species known to humanity.

Why on God's green earth would anyone attempt to persuade us to believe anything so preposterous or contrary to reason? Society views this act as it truly is: grossly immoral and unnatural behavior. If you ever were to permit this activity within our society, the wall of defense would be demolished into a pile of rubble. Acts of greater perversion would become the next hole to excavate until possibly we could dig ourselves right into hell itself and meet the instigator of all evil itself. Sorry, no way, no how, no, not ever. As far as I'm concerned, not a chance on God's green earth!

CONCLUSION

As Americans and citizens of this great nation we all share a common duty to participate in our civil responsibility in the electoral process. Trends within our society will come and they will go. When very dangerous and illicit actions threaten the very foundations of our conscience and country's civility, we must act decisively and deliberately to cease those actions. To do otherwise will ensure the establishment of lawlessness, licentiousness and instability within our populous. There exist standards of right and wrong for all of mankind. To ignore those standards, or worse yet to reject these standards, is in effect willfully participating in these wrongful acts as accomplices and becoming a party in this wrongdoing. We cannot ignore the implications.

Our laws are construed of this very notion and many people who have not directly committed any crime, but knowingly sat back and witnessed it being committed, are found guilty by association for merely knowing of the intended act of criminal intent and not being willing to act in opposition to the infraction or violation.

This issue of "homosexual union" or individuals of the same sex being married has no place in a civilized society, or basis of reason to be introduced in a culture where standards of right and wrong exist. It not only defies our laws, it is the utter disregard of reason and logic.

Fundamentally I view with antipathy the mere notion of introducing this into American culture as a "norm" because it is absolutely unacceptable behavior. This transgender or sexually deviant group has always existed and will continue to exist. This is not the question they seek the answer to! This group wants our approval, advocacy and acceptance by insisting that we, the 96 percent of Americans who choose to not participate in this brazen effort to sanctify inappropriate actions and behavior we find extremely offensive, unconscionable and reprehensible.

In order that this should change our minds and hearts forcing us to embrace this lifestyle nationally and allow this deviant alternate behavior to become acceptable within our society, thereby including in our nation's public school system this inordinate practice of indecency. As of 2016 it is now taught to every student in America from K-12 grade! What say you, America? These folks, through Obama's corrupt LGBT judges, have introduced through judicial caveat, curricula into your children's school, informing your children of this option to choose their gender. So if Susie comes home one day and tells you she is changing her name to Bill–what will you do then?

Be sure and thank Obama who is responsible for this action through the National Education Association/Union, a nonprofit organization initiating this curricula policy into America's public school system as of 2016. This initiative has not been approved or passed in either house of Congress. Now is the time for action to remove and protect our children from this dangerous attempt to allow this gross misconduct and act of invasion into American society, behavior that has been considered totally unacceptable within any culture for thousands of years. To allow this degenerate pattern of behavior to continue will surely result in disaster.

Tim Chipps has made his profession in the construction industry for the past 40 years. The father of 19 children, he resides in Alaska with his wife and family.

APPENDIX

Thanksgiving Proclamation

Issued by President George Washington, at the request of Congress on October 3, 1789

Whereas it is the duty of all nations to acknowledge the providence of Almighty God, to obey His will, to be grateful for His benefits, and humbly to implore His protection and favor; and—Whereas both Houses of Congress have, by their joint committee, requested me "to recommend to the people of the United States a day of public thanksgiving and prayer to be observed by acknowledging with grateful hearts the many and signal favors of Almighty God, especially by affording them an opportunity peaceably to establish a form of government for their safety and happiness.." ,Now, therefore, I do recommend and assign Thursday, the 26th day of November next, to be devoted by the people of these States to the service of that great and glorious Being who is the beneficent author of all the good that was, that is, or that will be; that we may unite in rendering unto Him our sincere and humble thanks for His kind care and protection of the people of this country previous to their becoming a nation; for the signal and manifold mercies and the favorable interpositions of His providence in the course and conclusion of the late war; for the great degree of tranquility, union, and plenty which we have since enjoyed; for the peaceable and rational manner in which we have been enabled to establish constitutions of government for our safety and happiness, and particularly the national one now lately instituted; for the civil and religious liberty with which we are blessed, and the means we have of acquiring and diffusing useful knowledge; and, in general, for all the great and various favors which

He has been pleased to confer upon us. And also that we may then unite in most humbly offering our prayers and supplications to the great Lord and Ruler of Nations, and beseech Him to pardon our national and other transgressions; to enable us all, whether in public or private stations, to perform our several and relative duties properly and punctually; to render our National Government a blessing to all the people by constantly being a Government of wise, just, and constitutional laws, discreetly and faithfully executed and obeyed; to protect and guide all sovereigns and nations (especially such as have shown kindness to us), and to bless them with good government, peace and concord; to promote the knowledge and practice of true religion and virtue, and the increase of science among them and us; and generally, to grant unto all mankind such a degree of temporal prosperity as He alone knows to be best.

Given under my hand at the City of New York the third day of October in the year of our Lord 1789.
(George Washington)

President George Washington

Declaration of Independence

IN CONGRESS, July 4, 1776.

The unanimous Declaration of the thirteen united States of America,

When in the Course of human events, it becomes necessary for one people to dissolve the political bands which have connected them with another, and to assume among the powers of the earth, the separate and equal station to which the Laws of Nature and of Nature's God entitle them, a decent respect to the opinions of mankind requires that they should declare the causes which impel them to the separation.

We hold these truths to be self-evident, that all men are created equal, that they are endowed by their Creator with certain unalienable Rights, that among these are Life, Liberty and the pursuit of Happiness.— That to secure these rights, Governments are instituted among Men, deriving their just powers from the consent of the governed,—That whenever any Form of Government becomes destructive of these ends, it is the Right of the People to alter or to abolish it, and to institute new Government, laying its foundation on such principles and organizing its powers in such form, as to them shall seem most likely to effect their Safety and Happiness. Prudence, indeed, will dictate that Governments long established should not be changed for light and transient causes; and accordingly all experience hath shewn, that mankind are more disposed to suffer, while evils are sufferable, than to right themselves by abolishing the forms to which they are accustomed. But when a long train of abuses and usurpations, pursuing invariably the same Object evinces a design to reduce them under absolute

Despotism, it is their right, it is their duty, to throw off such Government, and to provide new Guards for their future security.— Such has been the patient sufferance of these Colonies; and such is now the necessity which constrains them to alter their former Systems of Government. The history of the present King of Great Britain is a history of repeated injuries and usurpations, all having in direct object the establishment of an absolute Tyranny over these States. To prove this, let Facts be submitted to a candid world.

He has refused his Assent to Laws, the most wholesome and necessary for the public good.

He has forbidden his Governors to pass Laws of immediate and pressing importance, unless suspended in their operation till his Assent should be obtained; and when so suspended, he has utterly neglected to attend to them.

He has refused to pass other Laws for the accommodation of large districts of people, unless those people would relinquish the right of Representation in the Legislature, a right inestimable to them and formidable to tyrants only.

He has called together legislative bodies at places unusual, uncomfortable, and distant from the depository of their public Records, for the sole purpose of fatiguing them into compliance with his measures.

He has dissolved Representative Houses repeatedly, for opposing with manly firmness his invasions on the rights of the people.

He has refused for a long time, after such dissolutions, to cause others to be elected; whereby the Legislative powers, incapable of Annihilation, have returned to the People at large for their exercise; the State remaining in the mean time exposed to all the dangers of invasion from without, and convulsions within.

He has endeavoured to prevent the population of these States; for that purpose obstructing the Laws for Naturalization of Foreigners; refusing to pass others to encourage their migrations hither, and raising the conditions of new Appropriations of Lands.

He has obstructed the Administration of Justice, by refusing his Assent to Laws for establishing Judiciary powers.

He has made Judges dependent on his Will alone, for the tenure of their offices, and the amount and payment of their salaries.

He has erected a multitude of New Offices, and sent hither swarms of Officers to harass our people, and eat out their substance.

He has kept among us, in times of peace, Standing Armies without the Consent of our legislatures.

He has affected to render the Military independent of and superior to the Civil power.

He has combined with others to subject us to a jurisdiction foreign to our constitution, and unacknowledged by our laws; giving his Assent to their Acts of pretended Legislation:

For Quartering large bodies of armed troops among us:

For protecting them, by a mock Trial, from punishment for

any Murders which they should commit on the Inhabitants of these States:

For cutting off our Trade with all parts of the world:

For imposing Taxes on us without our Consent:

For depriving us in many cases, of the benefits of Trial by Jury:

For transporting us beyond Seas to be tried for pretended offences

For abolishing the free System of English Laws in a neighbouring Province, establishing therein an Arbitrary government, and enlarging its Boundaries so as to render it at once an example and fit instrument for introducing the same absolute rule into these Colonies:

For taking away our Charters, abolishing our most valuable Laws, and altering fundamentally the Forms of our Governments:

For suspending our own Legislatures, and declaring themselves invested with power to legislate for us in all cases whatsoever.

He has abdicated Government here, by declaring us out of his Protection and waging War against us.

He has plundered our seas, ravaged our Coasts, burnt our towns, and destroyed the lives of our people.

He is at this time transporting large Armies of foreign Mercenaries to compleat the works of death, desolation and tyranny, already begun with circumstances of Cruelty & perfidy scarcely paralleled in the most barbarous ages, and totally unworthy of the Head of a civilized nation.

He has constrained our fellow Citizens taken Captive on the high Seas to bear arms against their Country, to become the executioners of their friends and Brethren, or to fall themselves by their Hands.

He has excited domestic insurrections amongst us, and has endeavoured to bring on the inhabitants of our frontiers, the merciless Indian Savages, whose known rule of warfare, is an undistinguished destruction of all ages, sexes and conditions.

In every stage of these Oppressions We have Petitioned for Redress in the most humble terms: Our repeated Petitions have been answered only by repeated injury. A Prince whose character is thus marked by every act which may define a Tyrant, is unfit to be the ruler of a free people.

Nor have We been wanting in attentions to our Brittish brethren. We have warned them from time to time of attempts by their legislature to extend an unwarrantable jurisdiction over us. We have reminded them of the circumstances of our emigration and settlement here. We have appealed to their native justice and magnanimity, and we have conjured them by the ties of our common kindred to disavow these usurpations, which, would inevitably interrupt our connections and correspondence. They too have been deaf to the voice of justice and of consanguinity. We must, therefore, acquiesce in the necessity, which denounces our Separation, and hold them, as we hold the rest of mankind, Enemies in War, in Peace Friends.

We, therefore, the Representatives of the united States of America, in General Congress, Assembled, appealing to the Supreme Judge of the world for the rectitude of our intentions, do, in the Name, and by Authority of the good People of these Colonies, solemnly publish and declare, That these United Colonies are, and of Right ought to be Free and Independent States; that they are Absolved from all Allegiance to the British Crown, and that all political connection between them and the State of Great Britain, is and ought to be totally dissolved; and that as Free and Independent States, they have full Power to levy War, conclude Peace, contract Alliances, establish Commerce, and to do all other Acts and Things which Independent States may of right do. And for the support of this Declaration, with a firm reliance on the protection of divine Providence, we mutually pledge to each other our Lives, our Fortunes and our sacred Honor.

Georgia:
Button Gwinnett
Lyman Hall
George Walton
North Carolina:
William Hooper
Joseph Hewes
John Penn
South Carolina:
Edward Rutledge
Thomas Heyward, Jr.
Thomas Lynch, Jr.
Arthur Middleton
Massachusetts:
John Hancock
Maryland:
Samuel Chase
William Paca
Thomas Stone
Charles Carroll of Carrollton
Virginia:
George Wythe
Richard Henry Lee

Thomas Jefferson
Benjamin Harrison
Thomas Nelson, Jr.
Francis Lightfoot Lee
Carter Braxton
Pennsylvania:
Robert Morris
Benjamin Rush
Benjamin Franklin
John Morton
George Clymer
James Smith
George Taylor
James Wilson
George Ross
Delaware:
Caesar Rodney
George Read
Thomas McKean
New York:
William Floyd
Philip Livingston
Francis Lewis
Lewis Morris

New Jersey:
Richard Stockton
John Witherspoon
Francis Hopkinson
John Hart
Abraham Clark
New Hampshire:
Josiah Bartlett
William Whipple
Massachusetts:
Samuel Adams
John Adams
Robert Treat Paine
Elbridge Gerry
Rhode Island:
Stephen Hopkins
William Ellery
Connecticut:
Roger Sherman
Samuel Huntington
William Williams
Oliver Wolcott
New Hampshire:
Matthew Thornton

CONSTITUTION OF THE UNITED STATES

We the People of the United States, in Order to form a more perfect Union, establish Justice, insure domestic Tranquility, provide for the common defence, promote the general Welfare, and secure the Blessings of Liberty to ourselves and our Posterity, do ordain and establish this Constitution for the United States of America.

Article I.

Section 1. All legislative Powers herein granted shall be vested in a Congress of the United States, which shall consist of a Senate and House of Representatives.

Section 2. The House of Representatives shall be composed of Members chosen every second Year by the People of the several States, and the Electors in each State shall have the Qualifications requisite for Electors of the most numerous Branch of the State Legislature.

No Person shall be a Representative who shall not have attained to the age of twenty five Years, and been seven Years a Citizen of the United States, and who shall not, when elected, be an Inhabitant of that State in which he shall be chosen.

Representatives and direct Taxes shall be apportioned among the several States which may be included within this Union, according to their respective Numbers, which shall be determined by adding to the whole Number of free Persons, including those bound to Service for a Term of Years, and excluding Indians not taxed, three fifths of all other Persons. The actual Enumeration shall be made within three Years after the first Meeting of the Congress of the United States, and within every subsequent Term of ten Years, in such Manner as they shall by Law direct. The Number of Representatives shall not exceed one for every thirty Thousand, but each State shall have at Least one Representative; and until such enumeration shall be made, the State of New Hampshire shall be entitled to chuse three, Massachusetts eight, Rhode Island and Providence Plantations one, Connecticut five, New York six, New Jersey four, Pennsylvania eight, Delaware one, Maryland six, Virginia ten, North Carolina five, South Carolina five, and Georgia three.

When vacancies happen in the Representation from any State, the Executive Authority thereof shall issue Writs of Election to fill such Vacancies.

The House of Representatives shall chuse their Speaker and other Officers; and shall have the sole Power of Impeachment.

Section 3. The Senate of the United States shall be composed of two Senators from each State, chosen by the Legislature thereof, for six Years; and each Senator shall have one Vote.

Immediately after they shall be assembled in Consequence of the first Election, they shall be divided as equally as may be into three Classes. The Seats of the Senators of the first Class shall be vacated at the Expiration of the second Year, of the second Class at the Expiration of the fourth Year, and the third Class at the Expiration of the sixth Year, so that one third may be chosen every second Year; and if Vacancies happen by Resignation, or otherwise, during the Recess of the Legislature of any State, the Executive thereof may make temporary Appointments until the next Meeting of the Legislature, which shall then fill such Vacancies.

No Person shall be a Senator who shall not have attained to the Age of thirty Years, and been nine Years a Citizen of the

United States and who shall not, when elected, be an Inhabitant of that State for which he shall be chosen.

The Vice President of the United States shall be President of the Senate but shall have no Vote, unless they be equally divided.

The Senate shall chuse their other Officers, and also a President *pro tempore*, in the Absence of the Vice President, or when he shall exercise the Office of President of the United States.

The Senate shall have the sole Power to try all Impeachments. When sitting for that Purpose, they shall be on Oath or Affirmation. When the President of the United States is tried the Chief Justice shall preside: And no Person shall be convicted without the Concurrence of two thirds of the Members present.

Judgment in Cases of Impeachment shall not extend further than to removal from Office, and disqualification to hold and enjoy any Office of honor, Trust or Profit under the United States: but the Party convicted shall nevertheless be liable and subject to Indictment, Trial, Judgment and Punishment, according to Law.

Section 4. The Times, Places and Manner of holding Elections for Senators and Representatives, shall be prescribed in each State by the Legislature thereof; but the Congress may at any time by Law make or alter such Regulations, except as to the Places of chusing Senators.

The Congress shall assemble at least once in every Year, and such Meeting shall be on the first Monday in December, unless they shall by Law appoint a different Day.

Section 5. Each House shall be the Judge of the Elections, Returns and Qualifications of its own Members, and a Majority of each shall constitute a Quorum to do Business; but a smaller Number may adjourn from day to day, and may be authorized to compel the Attendance of absent Members, in such Manner, and under such Penalties as each House may provide.

Each House may determine the Rules of its Proceedings, punish its Members for disorderly Behaviour, and, with the Concurrence of two thirds, expel a Member.

Each House shall keep a Journal of its Proceedings, and from time to time publish the same, excepting such Parts as may in their Judgment require Secrecy; and the Yeas and Nays of the Members of either House on any question shall, at the Desire of one fifth of those Present, be entered on the Journal.

Neither House, during the Session of Congress, shall, without the Consent of the other, adjourn for more than three days, nor to any other Place than that in which the two Houses shall be sitting.

Section 6. The Senators and Representatives shall receive a Compensation for their Services, to be ascertained by Law, and paid out of the Treasury of the United States. They shall in all Cases, except Treason, Felony and Breach of the Peace, be privileged from Arrest during their Attendance at the Session of their respective Houses, and in going to and returning from the same; and for any Speech or Debate in either House, they shall not be questioned in any other Place.

No Senator or Representative shall, during the Time for which he was elected, be appointed to any civil Office under the Authority of the United States, which shall have been created, or the

Emoluments whereof shall have been encreased during such time; and no Person holding any Office under the United States, shall be a Member of either House during his Continuance in Office.

Section 7. All Bills for raising Revenue shall originate in the House of Representatives; but the Senate may propose or concur with amendments as on other Bills.

Every Bill which shall have passed the House of Representatives and the Senate, shall, before it become a law, be presented to the President of the United States: If he approve he shall sign it, but if not he shall return it, with his Objections to that House in which it shall have originated, who shall enter the Objections at large on their Journal, and proceed to reconsider it. If after such Reconsideration two thirds of that House shall agree to pass the Bill, it shall be sent, together with the Objections, to the other House, by which it shall likewise be reconsidered, and if approved by two thirds of that House, it shall become a Law. But in all such Cases the Votes of both Houses shall be determined by Yeas and Nays, and the Names of the Persons voting for and against the Bill shall be entered on the Journal of each House respectively. If any Bill shall not be returned by the President within ten Days (Sundays excepted) after it shall have been presented to him, the Same shall be a Law, in like Manner as if he had signed it, unless the Congress by their Adjournment prevent its Return, in which Case it shall not be a Law

Every Order, Resolution, or Vote to which the Concurrence of the Senate and House of Representatives may be necessary (except on a question of Adjournment) shall be presented to the President of the United States; and before the Same shall take

Effect, shall be approved by him, or being disapproved by him, shall be repassed by two thirds of the Senate and House of Representatives, according to the Rules and Limitations prescribed in the Case of a Bill.

Section 8. The Congress shall have Power To lay and collect Taxes, Duties, Imposts and Excises, to pay the Debts and provide for the common Defence and general Welfare of the United States; but all Duties, Imposts and Excises shall be uniform throughout the United States;

To borrow Money on the credit of the United States;

To regulate Commerce with foreign Nations, and among the several States, and with the Indian Tribes;

To establish an uniform Rule of Naturalization, and uniform Laws on the subject of Bankruptcies throughout the United States;

To coin Money, regulate the Value thereof, and of foreign Coin, and fix the Standard of Weights and Measures;

To provide for the Punishment of counterfeiting the Securities and current Coin of the United States;

To establish Post Offices and post Roads;

To promote the Progress of Science and useful Arts, by securing for limited Times to Authors and Inventors the exclusive Right to their respective Writings and Discoveries;

To constitute Tribunals inferior to the supreme Court;

To define and punish Piracies and Felonies committed on the high Seas, and Offences against the Law of Nations;

To declare War, grant Letters of Marque and Reprisal, and make Rules concerning Captures on Land and Water;

To raise and support Armies, but no Appropriation of Money to that Use shall be for a longer Term than two Years;

To provide and maintain a Navy;

To make Rules for the Government and Regulation of the land and naval Forces;

To provide for calling forth the Militia to execute the Laws of the Union, suppress Insurrections and repel Invasions;

To provide for organizing, arming, and disciplining, the Militia, and for governing such Part of them as may be employed in the Service of the United States, reserving to the States respectively, the Appointment of the Officers, and the Authority of training the Militia according to the discipline prescribed by Congress;

To exercise exclusive Legislation in all Cases whatsoever, over such District (not exceeding ten Miles square) as may, by Cession of Particular States, and the Acceptance of Congress, become the seat of the Government of the United States, and to exercise like Authority over all Places purchased by the Consent of the Legislature of the State in which the Same shall be, for the Erection of Forts, Magazines, Arsenals, dock-Yards, and other needful Buildings;—And

To make all Laws which shall be necessary and proper for carrying into Execution the foregoing Powers, and all other Powers vested by this Constitution in the Government of the United States, or in any Department or Officer thereof.

Section 9. The Migration or Importation of such Persons as any of the States now existing shall think proper to admit, shall not be prohibited by the Congress prior to the Year one thousand eight hundred and eight, but a Tax or duty may be imposed on such Importation, not exceeding ten dollars for each Person.

The Privilege of the Writ of *Habeas Corpus* shall not be suspended, unless when in Cases or Rebellion or Invasion the public Safety may require it.

No Bill of Attainder or *ex post facto* Law shall be passed.

No Capitation, or other direct, Tax shall be laid, unless in the Proportion to the Census of Enumeration herein before directed to be taken.

No Tax or Duty shall be laid on Articles exported from any State.

No Preference shall be given by any Regulation of Commerce or Revenue to the Ports of one State over those of another: nor shall Vessels bound to, or from, one State, be obliged to enter, clear or pay Duties in another.

No Money shall be drawn from the Treasury, but in Consequence of Appropriations made by Law; and a regular Statement and Account of the Receipts and Expenditures of all public Money shall be published from time to time.

No Title of Nobility shall be granted by the United States: and no Person holding any Office of Profit or Trust under them, shall, without the Consent of the Congress, accept of any present, Emolument, Office, or Title, of any kind whatever, from any King, Prince, or foreign State.

Section 10. No State shall enter into any Treaty, Alliance, or Confederation; grant Letters of Marque and Reprisal; coin Money; emit Bills of Credit; make any Thing but gold and silver Coin a Tender in Payment of Debts; pass any Bill of Attainder, *ex post facto* Law, or Law impairing the Obligation of Contracts, or grant any Title of Nobility.

No State shall, without the Consent of the Congress, lay any Imposts or Duties on Imports or Exports, except what may be absolutely necessary for executing it's inspection Laws: and the net Produce of all Duties and Imposts, laid by any State on Imports or Exports, shall be for the Use of the Treasury of the United States; and all such Laws shall be subject to the Revision and Controul of the Congress.

No State shall, without the Consent of Congress, lay any Duty of Tonnage, keep Troops, or Ships of War in time of Peace, enter into any Agreement or Compact with another State, or with a foreign Power, or engage in War, unless actually invaded, or in such imminent Danger as will not admit of delay.

Article II.

Section 1. The executive Power shall be vested in a President of the United States of America. He shall hold his Office during the Term of four Years, and, together with the Vice President, chosen for the same Term, be elected, as follows:

Each State shall appoint, in such Manner as the Legislature thereof may direct, a Number of Electors, equal to the whole Number of Senators and Representatives to which the State may be entitled in the Congress: but no Senator or Representative, or Person holding an Office of Trust or Profit under the United States, shall be appointed an Elector.

The Electors shall meet in their respective States, and vote by Ballot for two Persons, of whom one at least shall not be an Inhabitant of the same State with themselves. And they shall make a List of all the Persons voted for, and of the Number of Votes for each; which List they shall sign and certify, and transmit sealed to the Seat of the Government of the United States, directed to the President of the Senate. The President of the Senate shall, in the Presence of the Senate and House of Representatives, open all the Certificates, and the Votes shall then be counted. The Person having the greatest Number of Votes shall be the President, if such Number be a Majority of the whole Number of Electors appointed; and if there be more than one who have such Majority, and have an equal Number of Votes, then the House of Representatives shall immediately chuse by Ballot one of them for President; and if no Person have a Majority, then from the five highest on the List the said House shall in like Manner chuse the President. But in chusing the President, the Votes shall be taken by States, the Representatives from each State having one Vote; a quorum for this Purpose shall consist of a Member or Members from two thirds of the States, and a Majority of all the States shall be necessary to a Choice. In every Case, after the Choice of the President, the Person having the greatest Number of Votes of the Electors shall be the Vice President. But if there should remain two or more who have equal Votes, the Senate shall chuse from them by Ballot the Vice President.

The Congress may determine the Time of chusing the Electors, and the Day on which they shall give their Votes; which Day shall be the same throughout the United States.

No Person except a natural born Citizen, or a Citizen of the United States, at the time of the Adoption of this Constitution, shall be eligible to the Office of President; neither shall any person be eligible to that Office who shall not have attained to the Age of thirty five Years, and been fourteen Years a Resident within the United States.

In Case of the Removal of the President from Office, or of his Death, Resignation, or Inability to discharge the Powers and

Duties of the said Office, the Same shall devolve on the Vice President, and the Congress may by Law provide for the Case of Removal, Death, Resignation or Inability, both of the President and Vice President, declaring what Officer shall then act as President, and such Officer shall act accordingly, until the Disability be removed, or a President shall be elected.

The President shall, at stated Times, receive for his Services, a Compensation, which shall neither be encreased nor diminished during the Period for which he shall have been elected, and he shall not receive within that Period any other Emolument from the United States, or any of them.

Before he enter on the Execution of his Office, he shall take the following Oath or Affirmation:—"I do solemnly swear (or affirm) that I will faithfully execute the Office of President of the United States, and will to the best of my Ability, preserve, protect and defend the Constitution of the United States."

Section 2. The President shall be Commander in Chief of the Army and Navy of the United States, and of the Militia of the several States, when called into the actual Service of the United States; he may require the Opinion, in writing, of the principal Officer in each of the executive Departments, upon any Subject relating to the Duties of their respective Offices, and he shall have Power to Grant Reprieves and Pardons for Offences against the United States, except in Cases of Impeachment.

He shall have Power, by and with the Advice and Consent of the Senate, to make Treaties, provided two thirds of the Senators present concur; and he shall nominate, and by and with the Advice and Consent of the Senate, shall appoint Ambassadors, other public Ministers and Consuls, Judges of the supreme Court, and all other Officers of the United States, whose Appointments are not herein otherwise provided for, and which shall be established by Law: but the Congress may by Law vest the Appointment of such inferior Officers, as they think proper, in the President alone, in the Courts of Law, or in the Heads of Departments.

The President shall have Power to fill up all Vacancies that may happen during the Recess of the Senate, by granting Commissions which shall expire at the End of their next Session.

Section 3. He shall from time to time give to the Congress Information on the State of the Union, and recommend to their Consideration such Measures as he shall judge necessary and expedient; he may, on extraordinary Occasions, convene both Houses, or either of them, and in Case of Disagreement between them, with Respect to the Time of Adjournment, he may adjourn them to such Time as he shall think proper; he shall receive Ambassadors and other public Ministers; he shall take Care that the Laws be faithfully executed, and shall Commission all the Officers of the United States.

Section 4. The President, Vice President and all Civil Officers of the United States, shall be removed from Office on Impeachment for and Conviction of, Treason, Bribery, or other high Crimes and Misdemeanors.

Article III.

Section 1. The judicial Power of the United States, shall be vested in one supreme Court, and in such inferior Courts as the Congress may from time to time ordain and establish. The Judges, both of the supreme and inferior Courts, shall hold their Offices during good Behaviour, and shall, at stated Times, receive for their Services, a Compensation, which shall not be diminished during their Continuance in Office.

Section 2. The judicial Power shall extend to all Cases, in Law and Equity, arising under this Constitution, the Laws of the United States, and Treaties made, or which shall be made, under their Authority;—to all Cases affecting Ambassadors, other public ministers and Consuls;—to all Cases of admiralty and maritime Jurisdiction;—to Controversies to which the United States shall be a Party;—to Controversies between two or more States;— between a State and Citizens of another State;— between Citizens of different States;—between Citizens of the same State claiming Lands under Grants of different States, and between a State, or the Citizens thereof, and foreign States, Citizens or Subjects.

In all Cases affecting Ambassadors, other public Ministers and Consuls, and those in which a State shall be Party, the supreme Court shall have original Jurisdiction. In all the other Cases before mentioned, the supreme Court shall have appellate Jurisdiction, both as to Law and Fact, with such Exceptions, and under such Regulations as the Congress shall make.

The Trial of all Crimes, except in Cases of Impeachment, shall be by Jury; and such Trial shall be held in the State where the said Crimes shall have been committed; but when not committed within any State, the Trial shall be at such Place or Places as the Congress may by Law have directed.

Section 3. Treason against the United States, shall consist only in levying War against them, or in adhering to their Enemies, giving them Aid and Comfort. No Person shall be convicted of Treason unless on the Testimony of two Witnesses to the same overt Act, or on Confession in open Court.

The Congress shall have Power to declare the Punishment of Treason, but no Attainder of Treason shall work Corruption of Blood, or Forfeiture except during the Life of the Person attainted.

Article IV.

Section 1. Full Faith and Credit shall be given in each State to the public Acts, Records, and judicial Proceedings of every other State. And the Congress may by general Laws prescribe the Manner in which such Acts, Records, and Proceedings shall be proved, and the Effect thereof.

Section 2. The Citizens of each State shall be entitled to all Privileges and Immunities of Citizens in the several States.

A Person charged in any State with Treason, Felony, or other Crime, who shall flee from Justice, and be found in another State, shall on Demand of the executive Authority of the State from which he fled, be delivered up, to be removed to the State having Jurisdiction of the Crime.

No Person held to Service or Labour in one State, under the Laws thereof, escaping into another, shall, in Consequence of any Law or Regulation therein, be discharged from such Service or Labour, but shall be delivered up on Claim of the Party to whom such Service or Labour may be due.

Section 3. New States may be admitted by the Congress into this Union; but no new State shall be formed or erected within the Jurisdiction of any other State; nor any State be formed by the Junction of two or more States, or Parts of States, without the Consent of the Legislatures of the States concerned as well as of the Congress.

The Congress shall have Power to dispose of and make all needful Rules and Regulations respecting the Territory or other Property belonging to the United States; and nothing in this Constitution shall be so construed as to Prejudice any Claims of the United States, or of any particular State.

Section 4. The United States shall guarantee to every State in this Union a Republican Form of Government, and shall protect each of them against Invasion; and on Application of the Legislature, or of the Executive (when the Legislature cannot be convened) against domestic Violence.

Article V.

The Congress, whenever two thirds of both Houses shall deem it necessary, shall propose Amendments to this Constitution, or, on the Application of the Legislatures of two thirds of the several States, shall call a Convention for proposing Amendments, which, in either Case, shall be valid to all Intents and Purposes, as Part of this Constitution, when ratified by the Legislatures of three fourths of the several States, or by Conventions in three fourths thereof, as the one or the other Mode of Ratification may be proposed by the Congress; Provided that no Amendment which may be made prior to the Year One thousand eight hundred and eight shall in any Manner affect the first and fourth Clauses in the Ninth Section of the first Article; and that no State, without its Consent, shall be deprived of its equal Suffrage in the Senate.

Article VI.

All Debts contracted and Engagements entered into, before the Adoption of this Constitution, shall be as valid against the United States under this Constitution, as under the Confederation.

This Constitution, and the Laws of the United States which shall be made in Pursuance thereof; and all Treaties made, or which shall be made, under the Authority of the United States, shall be the supreme Law of the Land; and the Judges in every State shall be bound thereby, any Thing in the Constitution or Laws of any state to the Contrary notwithstanding.

The Senators and Representatives before mentioned, and the Members of the several State Legislatures, and all executive and judicial Officers, both of the United States and of the several States, shall be bound by Oath or Affirmation, to support this Constitution; but no religious Test shall ever be required as a Qualification to any Office or public Trust under the United States.

Article VII.

The Ratification of the Conventions of nine States, shall be sufficient for the Establishment of this Constitution between the States so ratifying the same.

The Word, "the," being interlined between the seventh and eighth Lines of the first Page, The Word "Thirty" being partly written on an Erazure in the fifteenth Line of the first Page, The Words "is tried" being interlined between the thirty second and thirty third Lines of the first Page and the Word "the" being interlined between the forty third and forty fourth Lines of the second Page.

Attest WILLIAM JACKSON
Secretary

done in Convention by the Unanimous Consent of the States present the Seventeenth Day of September in the Year of our Lord one thousand seven hundred and Eighty seven and of the Independance of the United States of America the Twelfth. In witness whereof We have hereunto subscribed our Names,

Gº. WASHINGTON—Presidᵗ.
and deputy from Virginia

New Hampshire   JOHN LANGDON
                 NICHOLAS GILMAN

Massachusetts   NATHANIEL GORHAM
                 RUFUS KING

| Connecticut | Wᵐ Samˡ Johnson |
| | Roger Sherman |

New York . . . . ALEXANDER HAMILTON

New Jersey	Wil: Livingston
	David Brearley.
	Wᵐ Patterson.
	Jona: Dayton

Pennsylvania	B Franklin
	Thomas Mifflin
	Robᵗ Morris
	Geo. Clymer
	Thoˢ FitzSimons
	Jared Ingersol
	James Wilson
	Gouv Morris

Delaware	Geo: Read
	Gunning Bedford Jun
	John Dickinson
	Richard Bassett
	Jaco: Broom

Maryland	James McHenry
	Dan of Sᵗ Thoˢ Jenifer
	Danˡ Carroll

| Virginia | John Blair— |
| | James Madison Jr. |

North Carolina	Wᵐ Blount
	Richᵈ Dobbs Spaight
	Hu Williamson

South Carolina	J. Rutledge
	Charles Cotesworth Pinckney
	Charles Pinckney
	Pierce Butler

| Georgia | William Few |
| | Abr Baldwin |

In Convention Monday, September 17th 1787.

Present

The States of

New Hampshire, Massachusetts, Connecticut, Mr Hamilton from New York, New Jersey, Pennsylvania, Delaware, Maryland, Virginia, North Carolina, South Carolina and Georgia.

Resolved,

That the preceeding Constitution be laid before the United States in Congress assembled, and that it is the Opinion of this Convention, that it should afterwards be submitted to a Convention of Delegates, chosen in each State by the People thereof, under the Recommendation of its Legislature, for their Assent and Ratification; and that each Convention assenting to, and ratifying the Same, should give Notice thereof to the United States in Congress assembled. Resolved, That it is the Opinion of this Convention, that as soon as the Conventions of nine States shall have ratified this Constitution, the United States in Congress assembled should fix a Day on which Electors should be appointed by the States which shall have ratified the same, and a Day on which the Electors should assemble to vote for the President, and the Time and Place for commencing Proceedings under this Constitution. That after such Publication the Electors should be appointed, and the Senators and Representatives elected: That the Electors should meet on the Day fixed for the Election of the President, and should transmit their Votes certified, signed, sealed and directed, as the Constitution requires, to the Secretary of the United States in Congress assembled, that the Senators and Representatives should convene at the Time and Place assigned; that the Senators should appoint a President of the Senate, for the sole Purpose of receiving, opening and counting the Votes for President; and, that after he shall be chosen, the Congress, together with the President, should, without Delay, proceed to execute this Constitution.

By the Unanimous Order of the Convention

G°: WASHINGTON—Presid^t.

W. JACKSON Secretary.

The Bill of Rights—Simplified

The first ten amendments to the Constitution are commonly known as The Bill of Rights. The following is a simplified version of the Bill of Rights.

First Amendment
Freedom of Religion, Speech, Press, Assembly, Right to Petition

Second Amendment
Right to keep and bear arms

Third Amendment
No quartering of soldiers

Fourth Amendment
Freedom from unreasonable searches and seizures

Fifth Amendment
Right to due process of law, freedom from self-incrimination, double jeopardy

Sixth Amendment
Rights of accused persons, e.g., right to a speedy and public trial

Seventh Amendment
Right of trial by jury in civil cases

Eighth Amendment
Freedom from excessive bail, cruel and unusual punishments

Ninth Amendment
Other rights of the people

Tenth Amendment
Powers reserved to the states

The Amendments

The following are the Amendments to the Constitution. The first ten Amendments collectively are commonly known as the Bill of Rights.

Amendment 1 - Freedom of Religion, Press, Expression. Ratified 12/15/1791.

Congress shall make no law respecting an establishment of religion, or prohibiting the free exercise thereof; or abridging the freedom of speech, or of the press; or the right of the people peaceably to assemble, and to petition the Government for a redress of grievances.

Amendment 2 - Right to Bear Arms. Ratified 12/15/1791.

A well regulated Militia, being necessary to the security of a free State, the right of the people to keep and bear Arms, shall not be infringed.

Amendment 3 - Quartering of Soldiers. Ratified 12/15/1791.

No Soldier shall, in time of peace be quartered in any house, without the consent of the Owner, nor in time of war, but in a manner to be prescribed by law.

Amendment 4 - Search and Seizure. Ratified 12/15/1791.

The right of the people to be secure in their persons, houses, papers, and effects, against unreasonable searches and seizures, shall not be violated, and no Warrants shall issue, but upon probable cause, supported by Oath or affirmation, and particularly describing the place to be searched, and the persons or things to be seized.

Amendment 5 - Trial and Punishment, Compensation for Takings. Ratified 12/15/1791.

No person shall be held to answer for a capital, or otherwise infamous crime, unless on a presentment or indictment of a Grand Jury, except in cases arising in the land or naval forces, or in the Militia, when in actual service in time of War or public danger; nor shall any person be subject for the same offense to be twice put in jeopardy of life or limb; nor shall be compelled in any criminal case to be a witness against himself, nor be deprived of life, liberty, or property, without due process of law; nor shall private property be taken for public use, without just compensation.

Amendment 6 - Right to Speedy Trial, Confrontation of Witnesses. Ratified 12/15/1791.

In all criminal prosecutions, the accused shall enjoy the right to a speedy and public trial, by an impartial jury of the State and district wherein the crime shall have been committed, which district shall have been previously ascertained by law, and to be informed of the nature and cause of the accusation; to be confronted with the witnesses against him; to have compulsory process for obtaining witnesses in his favor, and to have the Assistance of Counsel for his defence.

Amendment 7 - Trial by Jury in Civil Cases. Ratified 12/15/1791.

In Suits at common law, where the value in controversy shall exceed twenty dollars, the right of trial by jury shall be preserved, and no fact tried by a jury, shall be otherwise re-examined in any Court of the United States, than according to the rules of the common law.

Amendment 8 - Cruel and Unusual Punishment. Ratified 12/15/1791.

Excessive bail shall not be required, nor excessive fines imposed, nor cruel and unusual punishments inflicted.

Amendment 9 - Construction of Constitution. Ratified 12/15/1791.

The enumeration in the Constitution, of certain rights, shall not be construed to deny or disparage others retained by the people.

Amendment 10 - Powers of the States and People. Ratified 12/15/1791.

The powers not delegated to the United States by the Constitution, nor prohibited by it to the States, are reserved to the States respectively, or to the people.

Amendment 11 - Judicial Limits. Ratified 2/7/1795.

The Judicial power of the United States shall not be construed to extend to any suit in law or equity, commenced or prosecuted against one of the United States by Citizens of another State, or by Citizens or Subjects of any Foreign State.

Amendment 12 - Choosing the President, Vice-President. Ratified 6/15/1804.

The Electors shall meet in their respective states, and vote by ballot for President and Vice-President, one of whom, at least, shall not be an inhabitant of the same state with themselves; they shall name in their ballots the person voted for as President, and in distinct ballots the person voted for as Vice-President, and they shall make distinct lists of all persons voted for as President, and of all persons voted for as Vice-President and of the number of votes for each, which lists they shall sign and certify, and transmit sealed to the seat of the government of the United States, directed to the President of the Senate;

The President of the Senate shall, in the presence of the Senate and House of Representatives, open all the certificates and the votes shall then be counted;

The person having the greatest Number of votes for President, shall be the President, if such number be a majority of the whole number of Electors appointed; and if no person have such majority, then from the persons having the highest numbers not exceeding three on the list of those voted for as President, the House of Representatives shall choose immediately, by ballot, the President. But in choosing the President, the votes shall be taken by states, the representation from each state having one vote; a quorum for this purpose shall consist of a member or members from two-thirds of the states, and a majority of all the states shall be necessary to a choice. And if the House of Representatives shall not choose a President whenever the right of choice shall devolve upon them, before the fourth day of March next following, then the Vice-President shall act as President, as in the case of the death or other constitutional disability of the President.

The person having the greatest number of votes as Vice-President, shall be the Vice-President, if such number be a majority of the whole number of Electors appointed, and if no person have a majority, then from the two highest numbers on the list, the Senate shall choose the Vice-President; a quorum for the purpose shall consist of two-thirds of the whole number of Senators, and a majority of the whole number shall be necessary to a choice. But no person constitutionally ineligible to the office of President shall be eligible to that of Vice-President of the United States.

Amendment 13 - Slavery Abolished. Ratified 12/6/1865.

1. Neither slavery nor involuntary servitude, except as a punishment for crime whereof the party shall have been duly convicted, shall exist within the United States, or any place subject to their jurisdiction.

2. Congress shall have power to enforce this article by appropriate legislation.

Amendment 14 - Citizenship Rights. Ratified 7/9/1868.

1. All persons born or naturalized in the United States, and subject to the jurisdiction thereof, are citizens of the United States and of the State wherein they reside. No State shall make or enforce any law which shall abridge the privileges or immunities of citizens of the United States; nor shall any State deprive any person of life, liberty, or property, without due process of law; nor deny to any person within its jurisdiction the equal protection of the laws.

2. Representatives shall be apportioned among the several States according to their respective numbers, counting the whole number of persons in each State, excluding Indians not taxed. But when the right to vote at any election for the choice of electors for President and Vice-President of the United States, Representatives in Congress, the Executive and Judicial officers of a State, or the members of the Legislature thereof, is denied to any of the male inhabitants of such State, being twenty-one years of age, and citizens of the United States, or in any way abridged, except for participation in rebellion, or other crime, the basis of representation therein shall be reduced in the proportion which the number of such male citizens shall bear to the whole number of male citizens twenty-one years of age in such State.

3. No person shall be a Senator or Representative in Congress, or elector of President and Vice-President, or hold any office, civil or military, under the United States, or under any State, who, having previously taken an oath, as a member of Congress, or as an officer of the United States, or as a member of any State legislature, or as an executive or judicial officer of any State, to support the Constitution of the United States, shall have engaged in insurrection or rebellion against the same, or given aid or comfort to the enemies thereof. But Congress may by a vote of two-thirds of each House, remove such disability.

4. The validity of the public debt of the United States, authorized by law, including debts incurred for payment of pensions and bounties for services in suppressing insurrection or rebellion, shall not be questioned. But neither the United States nor any State shall assume or pay any debt or obligation incurred in aid of insurrection or rebellion against the United States, or any claim for the loss or emancipation of any slave; but all such debts, obligations and claims shall be held illegal and void.

5. The Congress shall have power to enforce, by appropriate legislation, the provisions of this article.

Amendment 15 - Race No Bar to Vote. Ratified 2/3/1870.

1. The right of citizens of the United States to vote shall not be denied or abridged by the United States or by any State on account of race, color, or previous condition of servitude.

2. The Congress shall have power to enforce this article by appropriate legislation.

Amendment 16 - Status of Income Tax Clarified. Ratified 2/3/1913.

The Congress shall have power to lay and collect taxes on incomes, from whatever source derived, without apportionment among the several States, and without regard to any census or enumeration.

Amendment 17 - Senators Elected by Popular Vote. Ratified 4/8/1913.

The Senate of the United States shall be composed of two Senators from each State, elected by the people thereof, for six years; and each Senator shall have one vote. The electors in each State shall have the qualifications requisite for electors of the most numerous branch of the State legislatures.

When vacancies happen in the representation of any State in the Senate, the executive authority of such State shall issue writs of election to fill such vacancies: Provided, That the legislature of any State may empower the executive thereof to make temporary appointments until the people fill the vacancies by election as the legislature may direct.

This amendment shall not be so construed as to affect the election or term of any Senator chosen before it becomes valid as part of the Constitution.

Amendment 18 - Liquor Abolished. Ratified 1/16/1919. Repealed by Amendment 21, 12/5/1933.

1. After one year from the ratification of this article the manufacture, sale, or transportation of intoxicating liquors within, the importation thereof into, or the exportation thereof from the United States and all territory subject to the jurisdiction thereof for beverage purposes is hereby prohibited.

2. The Congress and the several States shall have concurrent power to enforce this article by appropriate legislation.

3. This article shall be inoperative unless it shall have been ratified as an amendment to the Constitution by the legislatures of the several States, as provided in the Constitution, within seven years from the date of the submission hereof to the States by the Congress.

Amendment 19 - Women's Suffrage. Ratified 8/18/1920.

The right of citizens of the United States to vote shall not be denied or abridged by the United States or by any State on account of sex.

Congress shall have power to enforce this article by appropriate legislation.

Amendment 20 - Presidential, Congressional Terms. Ratified 1/23/1933.

1. The terms of the President and Vice President shall end at noon on the 20th day of January, and the terms of Senators and Representatives at noon on the 3d day of January, of the years in which such terms would have ended if this article had not been ratified; and the terms of their successors shall then begin.

2. The Congress shall assemble at least once in every year, and such meeting shall begin at noon on the 3d day of January, unless they shall by law appoint a different day.

3. If, at the time fixed for the beginning of the term of the President, the President elect shall have died, the Vice President elect shall become President. If a President shall not have been chosen before the time fixed for the beginning of his term, or if the President elect shall have failed to qualify, then the Vice President elect shall act as President until a President shall have qualified; and the Congress may by law provide for the case wherein neither a President elect nor a Vice President elect shall have qualified, declaring who shall then act as President, or the manner in which one who is to act shall be selected, and such person shall act accordingly until a President or Vice President shall have qualified.

4. The Congress may by law provide for the case of the death of any of the persons from whom the House of Representatives may choose a President whenever the right of choice shall have devolved upon them, and for the case of the death of any of the persons from whom the Senate may choose a Vice President whenever the right of choice shall have devolved upon them.

5. Sections 1 and 2 shall take effect on the 15th day of October following the ratification of this article.

6. This article shall be inoperative unless it shall have been ratified as an amendment to the Constitution by the legislatures of three-fourths of the several States within seven years from the date of its submission.

Amendment 21 - Amendment 18 Repealed. Ratified 12/5/1933.

1. The eighteenth article of amendment to the Constitution of the United States is hereby repealed.

2. The transportation or importation into any State, Territory, or possession of the United States for delivery or use therein of intoxicating liquors, in violation of the laws thereof, is hereby prohibited.

3. The article shall be inoperative unless it shall have been ratified as an amendment to the Constitution by conventions in the several States, as provided in the Constitution, within seven years from the date of the submission hereof to the States by the Congress.

Amendment 22 - Presidential Term Limits. Ratified 2/27/1951.

1. No person shall be elected to the office of the President more than twice, and no person who has held the office of President, or acted as President, for more than two years of a term to which some other person was elected President shall be elected to the office of the President more than once. But this Article shall not apply to any person holding the office of President, when this Article was proposed by the Congress, and shall not prevent any person who may be holding the office of President, or acting as President, during the term within which this Article becomes operative from holding the office of President or acting as President during the remainder of such term.

2. This article shall be inoperative unless it shall have been ratified as an amendment to the Constitution by the legislatures of three-fourths of the several States within seven years from the date of its submission to the States by the Congress.

Amendment 23 - Presidential Vote for District of Columbia. Ratified 3/29/1961.

1. The District constituting the seat of Government of the United States shall appoint in such manner as the Congress may direct: A number of electors of President and Vice President equal to the whole number of Senators and Representatives in Congress to which the District would be entitled if it were a State, but in no event more than the least populous State; they shall be in addition to those appointed by the States, but they shall be considered, for the purposes of the election of President and Vice President, to be electors appointed by a State; and they shall meet in the District and perform such duties as provided by the twelfth article of amendment.

2. The Congress shall have power to enforce this article by appropriate legislation.

Amendment 24 - Poll Tax Barred. Ratified 1/23/1964.

1. The right of citizens of the United States to vote in any primary or other election for President or Vice President, for electors for President or Vice President, or for Senator or Representative in Congress, shall not be denied or abridged by the United States or any State by reason of failure to pay any poll tax or other tax.

2. The Congress shall have power to enforce this article by appropriate legislation.

Amendment 25 - Presidential Disability and Succession. Ratified 2/10/1967.

1. In case of the removal of the President from office or of his death or resignation, the Vice President shall become President.

2. Whenever there is a vacancy in the office of the Vice President, the President shall nominate a Vice President who shall take office upon confirmation by a majority vote of both Houses of Congress.

3. Whenever the President transmits to the President pro tempore of the Senate and the Speaker of the House of Representatives his written declaration that he is unable to discharge the powers and duties of his office, and until he transmits to them a written declaration to the contrary, such powers and duties shall be discharged by the Vice President as Acting President.

4. Whenever the Vice President and a majority of either the principal officers of the executive departments or of such other body as Congress may by law provide, transmit to the President pro tempore of the Senate and the Speaker of the House of Representatives their written declaration that the President is unable to discharge the powers and duties of his office, the Vice President shall immediately assume the powers and duties of the office as Acting President.

Thereafter, when the President transmits to the President pro tempore of the Senate and the Speaker of the House of Representatives his written declaration that no inability exists, he shall resume the powers and duties of his office unless the Vice President and a majority of either the principal officers of the executive department or of such other body as Congress may by law provide, transmit within four days to the President pro tempore of the Senate and the Speaker of the House of Representatives their written declaration that the President is unable to discharge the powers and duties of his office. Thereupon Congress shall decide the issue, assembling within forty eight hours for that purpose if not in session. If the Congress, within twenty one days after receipt of the latter written declaration, or, if Congress is not in session, within twenty one days after Congress is required to assemble, determines by two thirds vote of both Houses that the President is unable to discharge the powers and duties of his office, the Vice President shall continue to discharge the same as Acting President; otherwise, the President shall resume the powers and duties of his office.

Amendment 26 - Voting Age Set to 18 Years. Ratified 7/1/1971.

1. The right of citizens of the United States, who are eighteen years of age or older, to vote shall not be denied or abridged by the United States or by any State on account of age.

2. The Congress shall have power to enforce this article by appropriate legislation.

Amendment 27 - Limiting Congressional Pay Increases. Ratified 5/7/1992.

No law, varying the compensation for the services of the Senators and Representatives, shall take effect, until an election of Representatives shall have intervened.

Senators of the 115th Congress

ALASKA

Murkowski, Lisa - (R - AK)
522 Hart Senate Office Building Washington DC 20510
(202) 224-6665
Contact: www.murkowski.senaate.gov/public/index.cfm/contact

Sullivan, Dan - (R - AK)
702 Hart Senate Office Building Washington DC 20510 (202) 224-3004
Contact: www.sullivan.senate.gov/contact/email

ALABAMA

Shelby, Richard C. - (R - AL)
304 Russell Senate Office Building Washington DC 20510
(202) 224-5744
Contact: www.shelby.senate.gov/public/index.cfm/emailsenatorshelby

Strange, Luther - (R - AL)
326 Russell Senate Office Building Washington DC 20510
(202) 224-4124
Contact: www.strange.senate.gov/content/contact-senator

ARKANSAS

Boozman, John - (R - AR)
141 Hart Senate Office Building Washington DC 20510
(202) 224-4843
Contact: www.boozman.senate.gov/public/index.cfm/contact

Cotton, Tom - (R - AR)
124 Russell Senate Office Building Washington DC 20510
(202) 224-2353
Contact: www.cotton.senate.gov/?p=contact

ARIZONA

Flake, Jeff - (R - AZ)
413 Russell Senate Office Building Washington DC 20510
(202) 224-4521
Contact: www.flake.senate.gov/public/index.cfm/contact-jeff

ARIZONA cont.

McCain, John - (R - AZ)
218 Russell Senate Office Building Washington DC 20510
(202) 224-2235
Contact: www.mccain.senate.gov/public/index.cfm/contact-form

CALIFORNIA

Feinstein, Dianne - (D - CA)
331 Hart Senate Office Building Washington DC 20510
(202) 224-3841
Contact: www.feinstein.senate.gov/public/index.cfm/e-mail-me

Harris, Kamala D. - (D - CA)
112 Hart Senate Office Building Washington DC 20510 (202) 224-3553
Contact: www.harris.senate.gov/content/contact-senator

COLORADO

Bennet, Michael F. - (D - CO)
261 Russell Senate Office Building Washington DC 20510
(202) 224-5852
Contact: www.bennet.senate.gov/?p=contact

Gardner, Cory - (R - CO)
354 Russell Senate Office Building Washington DC 20510
(202) 224-5941
Contact: www.gardner.senate.gov/contact-cory/email-cory

CONNECTICUT

Blumenthal, Richard - (D - CT)
706 Hart Senate Office Building Washington DC 20510
202) 224-2823
Contact: www.blumenthal.senate.gov/contact/

Murphy, Christopher - (D - CT)
136 Hart Senate Office Building Washington DC 20510 (202) 224-4041
Contact: www.murphy.senate.gov/contact

DELAWARE

Carper, Thomas R. - (D - DE)
513 Hart Senate Office Building Washington DC 20510
(202) 224-2441
Contact: www.carper.senate.gov/public/index.cfm/email-senator-carper

Coons, Christopher A. - (D - DE)
127A Russell Senate Office Building Washington DC 20510
(202) 224-5042
Contact: www.coons.senate.gov/contact

FLORIDA

Nelson, Bill - (D - FL)
716 Hart Senate Office Building Washington DC 20510
(202) 224-5274
Contact: www.billnelson.senate.gov/contact-bill

Rubio, Marco - (R - FL)
284 Russell Senate Office Building Washington DC 20510
(202) 224-3041
Contact: www.rubio.senate.gov/public/index.cfm/contact

GEORGIA

Isakson, Johnny - (R - GA)
131 Russell Senate Office Building Washington DC 20510
(202) 224-3643
Contact: www.isakson.senate.gov/public/index.cfm/email-me

Perdue, David - (R - GA)
455 Russell Senate Office Building Washington DC 20510
(202) 224-3521
Contact: www.perdue.senate.gov/connect/email

HAWAII

Hirono, Mazie K. - (D - HI)
730 Hart Senate Office Building Washington DC 20510 (202) 224-6361
Contact: www.hirono.senate.gov/contact

Schatz, Brian - (D - HI)
722 Hart Senate Office Building Washington DC 20510
(202) 224-3934
Contact: www.schatz.senate.gov/contact

IOWA

Ernst, Joni - (R - IA)
111 Russell Senate Office Building Washington DC 20510
(202) 224-3254
Contact: www.ernst.senate.gov/public/index.cfm/contact

IOWA cont.
Grassley, Chuck - (R - IA)
135 Hart Senate Office Building Washington DC 20510
(202) 224-3744
Contact: www.grassley.senate.gov/contact

IDAHO
Crapo, Mike - (R - ID)
239 Dirksen Senate Office Building Washington DC 20510
(202) 224-6142
Contact: www.crapo.senate.gov/contact

Risch, James E. - (R - ID)
483 Russell Senate Office Building Washington DC 20510
(202) 224-2752
Contact: www.risch.senate.gov/public/index.cfm?p=Email

ILLINOIS
Duckworth, Tammy - (D - IL)
524 Hart Senate Office Building Washington DC 20510
(202) 224-2854
Contact: www.duckworth.senate.gov/content/contact-senator

Durbin, Richard J. - (D - IL)
711 Hart Senate Office Building Washington DC 20510 (202) 224-2152
Contact: www.durbin.senate.gov/contact/

INDIANA
Donnelly, Joe - (D - IN)
720 Hart Senate Office Building Washington DC 20510
(202) 224-4814
Contact: www.donnelly.senate.gov/contact/email-joe

Young, Todd - (R - IN)
400 Russell Senate Office Building Washington DC 20510
(202) 224-5623
Contact: www.young.senate.gov/content/contact-senator

KANSAS
Moran, Jerry - (R - KS)
521 Dirksen Senate Office Building Washington DC 20510
(202) 224-6521
Contact: www.moran.senate.gov/public/index.cfm/e-mail-jerry

Roberts, Pat - (R - KS)
109 Hart Senate Office Building Washington DC 20510
(202) 224-4774
Contact: www.roberts.senate.gov/public/?p=EmailPat

KENTUCKY

McConnell, Mitch - (R - KY)
317 Russell Senate Office Building Washington DC 20510
(202) 224-2541
Contact: www.mcconnell.senate.gov/public/index.cfm?p=contact

Paul, Rand - (R - KY)
167 Russell Senate Office Building Washington DC 20510
(202) 224-4343
Contact: www.paul.senate.gov/connect/email-rand

LOUISIANA

Cassidy, Bill - (R - LA)
520 Hart Senate Office Building Washington DC 20510 (202) 224-5824
Contact: www.cassidy.senate.gov/contact

Kennedy, John - (R - LA)
383 Russell Senate Office Building Washington DC 20510
(202) 224-4623
Contact: www.kennedy.senate.gov/content/contact-senator

MASSACHUSETTS

Markey, Edward J. - (D - MA)
255 Dirksen Senate Office Building Washington DC 20510
(202) 224-2742
Contact: www.markey.senate.gov/contact

Warren, Elizabeth - (D - MA)
317 Hart Senate Office Building Washington DC 20510
(202) 224-4543
Contact: www.warren.senate.gov/?p=email_senator

MARYLAND

Cardin, Benjamin L. - (D - MD)
509 Hart Senate Office Building Washington DC 20510
(202) 224-4524
Contact: www.cardin.senate.gov/contact/

MARYLAND cont.

Van Hollen, Chris - (D - MD)
110 Hart Senate Office Building Washington DC 20510
(202) 224-4654
Contact: www.vanhollen.senate.gov/content/contact-senator

MAINE

Collins, Susan M. - (R - ME)
413 Dirksen Senate Office Building Washington DC 20510
(202) 224-2523
Contact: www.collins.senate.gov/contact

King, Angus S., Jr. - (I - ME)
133 Hart Senate Office Building Washington DC 20510
(202) 224-5344
Contact: www.king.senate.gov/contact

MICHIGAN

Peters, Gary C. - (D - MI)
724 Hart Senate Office Building Washington DC 20510
202) 224-6221
Contact: www.peters.senate.gov/contact/email-gary

Stabenow, Debbie - (D - MI)
731 Hart Senate Office Building Washington DC 20510
(202) 224-4822
Contact: www.stabenow.senate.gov/contact

MINNESOTA

Franken, Al - (D - MN)
309 Hart Senate Office Building Washington DC 20510
(202) 224-5641
Contact: www.franken.senate.gov/?p=contact

Klobuchar, Amy - (D - MN)
302 Hart Senate Office Building Washington DC 20510
(202) 224-3244
Contact: www.klobuchar.senate.gov/public/index.cfm/contact

MISSOURI

Blunt, Roy - (R - MO)
260 Russell Senate Office Building Washington DC 20510
(202) 224-5721
Contact: www.blunt.senate.gov/public/index.cfm/contact-roy

McCaskill, Claire - (D - MO)
503 Hart Senate Office Building Washington DC 20510
(202) 224-6154
Contact: www.mccaskill.senate.gov/contact

MISSISSIPPI

Cochran, Thad - (R - MS)
113 Dirksen Senate Office Building Washington DC 20510
(202) 224-5054
Contact: www.cochran.senate.gov/public/index.cfm/email-me

Wicker, Roger F. - (R - MS)
555 Dirksen Senate Office Building Washington DC 20510
(202) 224-6253
Contact: www.wicker.senate.gov/public/index.cfm/contact

MONTANA

Daines, Steve - (R - MT)
320 Hart Senate Office Building Washington DC 20510
(202) 224-2651
Contact: www.daines.senate.gov/connect/email-steve

Tester, Jon - (D - MT)
311 Hart Senate Office Building Washington DC 20510
(202) 224-2644
Contact: www.tester.senate.gov/?p=email_senator

NORTH CAROLINA

Burr, Richard - (R - NC)
217 Russell Senate Office Building Washington DC 20510
(202) 224-3154
Contact: www.burr.senate.gov/contact/email

Tillis, Thom - (R - NC)
185 Dirksen Senate Office Building Washington DC 20510
(202) 224-6342
Contact: www.tillis.senate.gov/public/index.cfm/email-me

NORTH DAKOTA

Heitkamp, Heidi - (D - ND)
516 Hart Senate Office Building Washington DC 20510
(202) 224-2043
Contact: www.heitkamp.senate.gov/public/index.cfm/contact

NORTH DAKOTA cont.

Hoeven, John - (R - ND)
338 Russell Senate Office Building Washington DC 20510
(202) 224-2551
Contact: www.hoeven.senate.gov/public/index.cfm/email-the-senator

NEBRASKA

Fischer, Deb - (R - NE)
454 Russell Senate Office Building Washington DC 20510
(202) 224-6551
Contact: www.fischer.senate.gov/public/index.cfm/contact

Sasse, Ben - (R - NE)
136 Russell Senate Office Building Washington DC 20510
(202) 224-4224
Contact: www.sasse.senate.gov/public/index.cfm/email-ben

NEW HAMPSHIRE

Hassan, Margaret Wood - (D - NH)
330 Hart Senate Office Building Washington DC 20510
(202) 224-3324
Contact: www.hassan.senate.gov/content/contact-senator

Shaheen, Jeanne - (D - NH)
506 Hart Senate Office Building Washington DC 20510
(202) 224-2841
Contact: www.shaheen.senate.gov/contact/contact-jeanne

NEW JERSEY

Booker, Cory A. - (D - NJ)
359 Dirksen Senate Office Building Washington DC 20510
(202) 224-3224
Contact: www.booker.senate.gov/?p=contact

Menendez, Robert - (D - NJ)
528 Hart Senate Office Building Washington DC 20510
(202) 224-4744
Contact: www.menendez.senate.gov/contact

NEW MEXICO

Heinrich, Martin - (D - NM)
303 Hart Senate Office Building Washington DC 20510
(202) 224-5521
Contact: www.heinrich.senate.gov/contact

Udall, Tom - (D - NM)
531 Hart Senate Office Building Washington DC 20510
(202) 224-6621
Contact: www.tomudall.senate.gov/?p=contact

NEVADA

Cortez Masto, Catherine - (D - NV)
204 Russell Senate Office Building Washington DC 20510
(202) 224-3542
Contact: www.cortezmasto.senate.gov/content/contact-senator

Heller, Dean - (R - NV)
324 Hart Senate Office Building Washington DC 20510
(202) 224-6244
Contact: www.heller.senate.gov/public/index.cfm/contact-form

NEW YORK

Gillibrand, Kirsten E. - (D - NY)
478 Russell Senate Office Building Washington DC 20510
(202) 224-4451
Contact: www.gillibrand.senate.gov/contact/

Schumer, Charles E. - (D - NY)
322 Hart Senate Office Building Washington DC 20510
(202) 224-6542
Contact: www.schumer.senate.gov/contact/email-chuck

OHIO

Brown, Sherrod - (D - OH)
713 Hart Senate Office Building Washington DC 20510
(202) 224-2315
Contact: www.brown.senate.gov/contact/

Portman, Rob - (R - OH)
448 Russell Senate Office Building Washington DC 20510
(202) 224-3353
Contact: www.portman.senate.gov/public/index.cfm/contact?p=contact...

OKLAHOMA

Inhofe, James M. - (R - OK)
205 Russell Senate Office Building Washington DC 20510
(202) 224-4721
Contact: www.inhofe.senate.gov/contact

OKLAHOMA cont.

Lankford, James - (R - OK)
316 Hart Senate Office Building Washington DC 20510
(202) 224-5754
Contact: www.lankford.senate.gov/contact/email

OREGON

Merkley, Jeff - (D - OR)
313 Hart Senate Office Building Washington DC 20510
(202) 224-3753
Contact: www.merkley.senate.gov/contact/

Wyden, Ron - (D - OR)
221 Dirksen Senate Office Building Washington DC 20510 (
202) 224-5244
Contact: www.wyden.senate.gov/contact/

PENNSYLVANIA

Casey, Robert P., Jr. - (D - PA)
393 Russell Senate Office Building Washington DC 20510
(202) 224-6324
Contact: www.casey.senate.gov/contact/

Toomey, Patrick J. - (R - PA)
248 Russell Senate Office Building Washington DC 20510
(202) 224-4254
Contact: www.toomey.senate.gov/?p=contact

RHODE ISLAND

Reed, Jack - (D - RI)
728 Hart Senate Office Building Washington DC 20510
(202) 224-4642
Contact: www.reed.senate.gov/contact/

Whitehouse, Sheldon - (D - RI)
530 Hart Senate Office Building Washington DC 20510
(202) 224-2921
Contact: www.whitehouse.senate.gov/contact/email-sheldon

SOUTH CAROLINA

Graham, Lindsey - (R - SC)
290 Russell Senate Office Building Washington DC 20510
(202) 224-5972
Contact: www.lgraham.senate.gov/public/index.cfm/e-mail-senator-gr...

Scott, Tim - (R - SC)
717 Hart Senate Office Building Washington DC 20510
(202) 224-6121
Contact: www.scott.senate.gov/contact/email-me

SOUTH DAKOTA

Rounds, Mike - (R - SD)
502 Hart Senate Office Building Washington DC 20510
(202) 224-5842
Contact: www.rounds.senate.gov/contact/email-mike

Thune, John - (R - SD)
511 Dirksen Senate Office Building Washington DC 20510
(202) 224-2321
Contact: www.thune.senate.gov/public/index.cfm/contact

TENNESSEE

Alexander, Lamar - (R - TN)
455 Dirksen Senate Office Building Washington DC 20510
(202) 224-4944
Contact: www.alexander.senate.gov/public/index.cfm?p=Email

Corker, Bob - (R - TN)
425 Dirksen Senate Office Building Washington DC 20510
(202) 224-3344
Contact: www.corker.senate.gov/public/index.cfm/emailme

TEXAS

Cornyn, John - (R - TX)
517 Hart Senate Office Building Washington DC 20510
(202) 224-2934
Contact: www.cornyn.senate.gov/contact

Cruz, Ted - (R - TX)
404 Russell Senate Office Building Washington DC 20510
(202) 224-5922
Contact: www.cruz.senate.gov/?p=email_senator

UTAH

Hatch, Orrin G. - (R - UT)
104 Hart Senate Office Building Washington DC 20510
(202) 224-5251
Contact: www.hatch.senate.gov/public/index.cfm/contact?p=Email-Orrin

UTAH cont.

Lee, Mike - (R - UT)
361A Russell Senate Office Building Washington DC 20510
(202) 224-5444
Contact: www.lee.senate.gov/public/index.cfm/contact

VIRGINIA

Kaine, Tim - (D - VA)
231 Russell Senate Office Building Washington DC 20510
(202) 224-4024
Contact: www.kaine.senate.gov/contact

Warner, Mark R. - (D - VA)
703 Hart Senate Office Building Washington DC 20510
(202) 224-2023
Contact: www.warner.senate.gov/public/index.cfm?p=Contact

VERMONT

Leahy, Patrick J. - (D - VT)
437 Russell Senate Office Building Washington DC 20510
(202) 224-4242
Contact: www.leahy.senate.gov/contact/

Sanders, Bernard - (I - VT)
332 Dirksen Senate Office Building Washington DC 20510
(202) 224-5141
Contact: www.sanders.senate.gov/contact/

WASHINGTON

Cantwell, Maria - (D - WA)
511 Hart Senate Office Building Washington DC 20510
(202) 224-3441
Contact: www.cantwell.senate.gov/public/index.cfm/email-maria

Murray, Patty - (D - WA)
154 Russell Senate Office Building Washington DC 20510
(202) 224-2621
Contact: www.murray.senate.gov/public/index.cfm/contactme

WISCONSIN

Baldwin, Tammy - (D - WI)
709 Hart Washington DC 20510
(202) 224-5653
Contact: www.baldwin.senate.gov/feedback

Johnson, Ron - (R - WI)
328 Hart Senate Office Building Washington DC 20510
(202) 224-5323
Contact: www.ronjohnson.senate.gov/public/index.cfm/email-the-sena...

WEST VIRGINIA

Capito, Shelley Moore - (R - WV)
172 Russell Senate Office Building Washington DC 20510
(202) 224-6472
Contact: www.capito.senate.gov/contact/contact-shelley

Manchin, Joe, III - (D - WV)
306 Hart Senate Office Building Washington DC 20510
(202) 224-3954
Contact: www.manchin.senate.gov/public/index.cfm/contact-form

WYOMING

Barrasso, John - (R - WY)
307 Dirksen Senate Office Building Washington DC 20510
(202) 224-6441
Contact: www.barrasso.senate.gov/public/index.cfm/contact-form

Enzi, Michael B. - (R - WY)
379A Russell Senate Office Building Washington DC 20510
(202) 224-3424
Contact: www.enzi.senate.gov/public/index.cfm/contact?p=e-mail-sen...

U. S. House of Representatives

Alabama

Rep. Jo Bonner (R-1st)
2236 Rayburn House Office Building
(202) 225-4931; 225-0562
Mobile: (334) 690-2811
Web Site

Rep. Martha Roby (R-2nd)
414 Cannon Office Building
(202) 225- 2901: 225-8913
Dothan: (334) 794-9680
Web Site

Rep. Michael Rogers (R-3rd)
324 Cannon House Office Building
(202) 225-3261; 226-8485
Anniston: (256) 236-5655
Web Site

Robert B. Aderholt (R-4th)
2264 Rayburn House Office Building
(202) 225-4876; 225-5587
Jasper: (205) 221-2310
Web Site

Rep. Mo Brooks (R-5th)
1641 Longworth House Office Building
(202) 225-4801; 225-4392
Huntsville: (256) 551-0190
Web Site

Rep. Spencer Bachus (R-6th)
2246 Rayburn House Office Building
(202) 225-4921; 226-2082
Birmingham: (205) 969-2296
Web Site

Rep. Terri Sewell (D-7th)
1133 Longworth House Office Building
(202) 225-2665; 226-9567
Birmingham: (205) 254-1960
Web Site

Alaska

Rep. Don Young (R-AL)
2314 Rayburn House Office Building
(202)225-5765; 225-0425
Anchorage: (907) 271-5978
Web Site

Amer'n Samoa

Del. Eni Faleomavaega (D-AL)
2422 Rayburn House Office Building
(202) 225-8577; 225-8757
Pago Pago: (684) 633-1372
Web Site

Arizona

Rep. Ann Kirkpatrick (D-1st) **
330 Cannon House Office Building
(202) 225-3361; 225-9739
Casa Grande: (520) 316-0839
Web Site

Rep. Ron Barber (D-2nd) **
1029 Longworth House Office Building
(202) 225-2542; 225-0378
Sierra Vista: (520) 459-3115
Web Site

Rep. Raul M. Grijalva (D-3rd)
1511 Longworth House Office Building
(202) 225-2435; 225-1541
Tucson: (520) 622-6788
Web Site

Rep. Paul Gosar (R-4th) **
504 Cannon House Office Building
(202) 225-2315; 225-9739
Prescott: (928) 445-1683
Web Site

Arizona cont.

Rep. Matt Salmon (R-5th) **
2349 Rayburn House Office Building
(202) 225-2635: 226-4386
Gilbert: (480) 699-8239

Rep. David Schweikert (R-6th)
1205 Longworth House Office Building
(202) 225-2190; 225-0096
Scottsdale: (480) 946-2411
Web Site

Rep. Ed Pastor (D-7th)
2465 Rayburn House Office Building
(202) 225-4065; 225-1655
Phoenix: (928) 256-0551
Web Site

Rep. Trent Franks (R-8th)
2435 Rayburn House Office Building
(202) 225-4576; 225-6328
Glendale: (623) 776-7911
Web Site

Rep. Kyrsten Sinema (D-9th) **
1237 Longworth House Office Building
(202) 225-9888; N/A
Phoenix: N/A
Web Site

Arkansas

Rep. Rick Crawford (R-1st)
1408 Longworth House Office Building
(202) 225-4076; 225-5602
Jonesboro: (870) 972-4600
Web Site

Rep. Tim Griffin (R-2nd)
1232 Longworth House Office Building
(202) 225-2506; 225-5903
Little Rock: (501) 324-5941
Web Site

Rep. Steve Womack (R-3rd)
1508 Longworth House Office Building
(202) 225-4301; 225-5713
Fort Smith: (479) 424-1146

Arkansas cont.

Rep. Tom Cotton (R-4th) **
415 Cannon House Office Building
(202) 225-3772; 225-1314
Pine Bluff: (870) 536-3376
Web Site

California

Rep. Doug LaMalfa (R-1st) **
506 Cannon House Office Building
(202) 225-3076; 226-0852
Oroville: N/A

Rep. Jared Huffman (D-2nd) **
1630 Longworth House Office Building
(202) 225-5161; N/A
Eureka: (707) 407-3585
Web Site

Rep. John Garamendi (D-3rd)
2438 Rayburn House Office Building
(202) 225-1880 ; 225-5914
Fairfield: (707) 438-1822
Web Site

Rep. Tom McClintock (R-4th)
428 Cannon House Office Building
(202) 225-2511; 225-5444
Granite Bay: (916) 786-5560
Web Site

Rep. Mike Thompson (D-5th)
231 Cannon House Office Building
(202) 225-3311; 225-4335
Napa: (707) 226-9898
Web Site

Rep. Doris Matsui (D-6th)
222 Cannon House Office Building
(202) 225-7163; 225-0566
Sacramento: (916) 498-5600
Web Site

Rep. Ami B. Bera (D-7th) **
1408 Longworth House Office Building
(202) 225-5716; 226-1298
N/A

California cont.

Rep. Paul Cook (R-8th) **
1222 Longworth House Office Building
(202) 225-5861; 225-6498
Apple Valley: N/A
Web Site

Rep. Jerry McNerney (D-9th)
1210 Longworth House Office Building
(202) 225-1947; 225-4060
Pleasanton: (925) 737-0727
Web Site

Rep. Jeff Denham (R-10th)
1730 Longworth House Office Building
(202) 225-4540; 225-3402
Modesto: (209) 579-5458
Web Site

Rep. George Miller (D-11th)
2205 Rayburn House Office Building
(202) 225-2095; 225-5609
Concord: (925) 602-1880
Web Site

Rep. Nancy Pelosi (D-12th)
235 Cannon House Office Building
(202) 225-4965; 225-8259
San Francisco: (415) 556-4862
Web Site

Rep. Barbara Lee (D-13th)
2267 Rayburn House Office Building
(202) 225-2661; 225-9817
Oakland: (510) 763-0370
Web Site

Rep. Jackie Speier (D-14th)
211 Cannon House Office Building
(202) 225-3531; 226-4183
San Mateo: (650) 342-0300
Web Site

Rep. Eric Swalwell (D-15th) **
501 Cannon House Office Building
(202) 225-5065; 226-3805
N/A
Web Site

California cont.

Rep. Jim Costa (D-16th)
1314 Longworth House Office Building
(202) 225-3341; 225-9308
Fresno: (559) 495-1620
Web Site

Rep. Mike Honda (D-17th)
1713 Longworth House Office Building
(202) 225-2631; 225-2699
Campbell: (408) 558-8085
Web Site

Rep. Anna Eshoo (D-18th)
205 Cannon House Office Building
(202) 225-8104; 225-8890
Palo Alto: (650) 323-2984
Web Site

Rep. Zoe Lofgren (D-19th)
1401 Longworth House Office Building
(202) 225-3072; 225-3336
San Jose: (408) 271-8700
Web Site

Rep. Sam Farr (D-20th)
1126 Longworth House Office Building
(202) 225-2861; 225-6791
Salinas: (831) 424-2229
Web Site

Rep. David Valadao (R-21st) **
1004 Longworth House Office Building
(202) 225-4695; 225-3196
Hanford: N/A
Web Site

Rep. Devin Nunes (R-22nd)
1013 Longworth House Office Building
(202) 225-2523; 225-3404
Visalia: (559) 733-3861
Web Site

Rep. Kevin McCarthy (R-23rd)
326 Cannon House Office Building
(202) 225-2915; 225-2908
Bakersfield: (661) 327-3611
Web Site

California cont.

Rep. Lois Capps (D-24th)
2231 Rayburn House Office Building
(202) 225-3601; 225-5632
Santa Barbara: (805) 730-1710
Web Site

Rep. Buck McKeon (R-25th)
2184 Rayburn House Office Building
(202) 225-1956; 226-0683
Santa Clarita: (805) 254-2111
Web Site

Rep. Julia Brownley (D-26th) **
1019 Longworth House Office Building
(202) 225-5811; 225-7018
N/A
Web Site

Rep. Judy Chu (D-27th)
1520 Longworth House Office Building
(202) 225-5464; 225-5467
El Monte: (626) 448-1271
Web Site

Rep. Adam Schiff (D-28th)
2411 Rayburn House Office Building
(202) 225-4176; 225-5828
Pasadena: (626) 304-2727
Web Site

Rep. Tony Cardenas (D-29th) **
1508 Longworth House Office Building
(202) 225-6131; 225-0819
N/A
Web Site

Rep. Brad Sherman (D-30th)
2242 Rayburn House Office Building
(202) 225-5911; 225-5879
Van Nuys: (818) 501-9200
Web Site

Rep. Gary Miller (R-31st)
2349 Rayburn House Office Building
(202) 225-3201; 226-6962
Brea: (714) 257-1142
Web Site

California cont.

Rep. Grace Napolitano (D-32nd)
1610 Longworth House Office Building
(202) 225-5256; 225-0027
Santa Fe Springs: (801) 801-2134
Web Site

Rep. Henry Waxman (D-33rd)
2204 Rayburn House Office Building
(202) 225-3976; 225-4099
Los Angeles: (323) 651-1040
Web Site

Rep. Xavier Becerra (D-34th)
1226 Longworth House Office Building
(202) 225-6235; 225-2202
Los Angeles: (213) 483-1425
Web Site

Rep. Gloria McLeod (D-35th) **
1641 Longworth House Office Building
(202) 225-6161; 225-8671
Montclair: (909) 626-2054
Web Site

Rep. Raul Ruiz (D-36th) **
1319 Longworth House Office Building
(202) 225-5330; 225-2961
Palm Springs: N/A
Web Site

Rep. Karen Bass (D-37th)
408 Cannon House Office Building
(202) 225-7084; 225-2422
Los Angeles: (323) 965-1422
Web Site

Rep. Linda Sanchez (D-38th)
2423 Rayburn House Office Building
(202) 225-6676; 226-1012
Cerritos: (562) 860-5050
Web Site

Rep. Ed Royce (R-39th)
2185 Rayburn House Office Building
(202) 225-4111; 226-0335
Orange: (714) 744-4130
Web Site

California cont.

Rep. Lucille Roybal-Allard (D-40th)
2330 Rayburn House Office Building
(202) 225-1766; 226-0350
Los Angeles: (213) 628-9230
Web Site

Rep. Mark Takano (D-41st) **
1507 Longworth House Office Building
(202) 225-2305; 225-7018
Riverside: N/A
Web Site

Rep. Ken Calvert (R-42nd)
2269 Rayburn House Office Building
(202) 225-1986; 225-2004
Riverside: (909) 784-4300
Web Site

Rep. Maxine Waters (D-43rd)
2344 Rayburn House Office Building
(202) 225-2201; 225-7854
Los Angeles: (213) 757-8900
Web Site

Rep. Janice Hahn (D-44th)
2400 Rayburn House Office Building
(202) 225-8220; 225-7290
Wilmington: (310) 549-8282
Web Site

Rep. John Campbell (R-45th)
1507 Longworth House Office Building
(202) 225-5611; 225-9177
Newport Beach: (949) 756-2244
Web Site

Rep. Loretta Sanchez (D-46th)
1114 Longworth House Office Building
(202) 225-2965; 225-5859
Garden Grove: (714) 621-0102
Web Site

Rep. Alan Lowenthal (D-47th) **
515 Cannon House Office Building
(202) 225-7924; 225-7926
Long Beach: (562) 436-3828
Web Site

California cont.

Rep. Dana Rohrabacher (R-48th)
2300 Rayburn House Office Building
(202) 225-2415; 225-0145
Huntington Beach: (714) 960-6483
Web Site

Rep. Darrell Issa (R-49th)
2347 Rayburn House Office Building
(202) 225-3906; 225-3303
Vista: (760) 599-5000
Web Site

Rep. Duncan Hunter (R-50th)
223 Cannon House Office Building
(202) 225-5672; 225-0235
El Cajon: (619) 448-5201
Web Site

Rep. Juan Vargas (D-51st) **
1605 Longworth House Office Building
(202) 225-8045; 225-9073
Chula Vista: (619) 422-5963
Web Site

Rep. Scott Peters (D-52nd) **
2410 Rayburn House Office Building
(202) 225-0508; 225-2558
N/A
Web Site

Rep. Susan Davis (D-53rd)
1526 Longworth House Office Building
(202) 225-2040; 225-2948
San Diego: (619) 280-5353
Web Site

Colorado

Rep. Diana DeGette (D-1st)
2335 Rayburn House Office Building
(202) 225-4431; 225-5657
Denver: (303) 844-4988
Web Site

Colorado cont.

Rep. Jared Polis (D-2nd)
501 Cannon House Office Building
(202) 225-2161; 226-7840
Boulder: (303) 484-9596
Web Site

Rep. Scott Tipton (R-3rd)
218 Cannon House Office Building
(202) 225-4761; 226-9669
Grand Junction: (970) 241-2499
Web Site

Rep. Cory Gardner (R-4th)
213 Cannon House Office Building
(202) 225-4676; 225-5870
Ft. Collins: (970) 221-7110
Web Site

Rep. Doug Lamborn (R-5th)
437 Cannon House Office Building
(202) 225-4422; 226-2638
Colorado Springs: (719) 520-0055
Web Site

Rep. Mike Coffman (R-6th)
1222 Longworth House Office Building
(202) 225-7882; 226-4623
Long Tree: (720) 283-9772
Web Site

Rep. Ed Perlmutter (D-7th)
1221 Longworth House Office Building
(202) 225-2645; 225-5278
Lakewood: (303) 274-7944
Web Site

Connecticut

Rep. John Larson (D-1st)
1501 Longworth House Office Building
(202) 225-2265; 225-1031
Hartford: (860) 278-8888

Conneticut cont.

Rep. Joseph Courtney (D-2nd)
215 Cannon House Office Building
(202) 225-2076; 225-4977
Norwich: (860) 886-0139
Web Site

Rep. Rosa DeLauro (D-3rd)
2413 Rayburn House Office Building
(202) 225-3661; 225-4890
New Haven: (203) 562-3718
Web Site

Rep. Jim Himes (D-4th)
119 Cannon House Office Building
(202) 225-5541; 225-9629
Bridgeport: (866) 453-0028
Web Site

Rep. Elizabeth Esty (D-5th) **
509 Cannon House Office Building
(202) 225-4476; 225-5933
New Britain: N/A
Web Site

Delaware

Rep. John Carney (D-AL)
1406 Longworth House Office Building
(202) 225-4165; 225-2291
Wilmington: (302) 691-7333
Web Site

District of Columbia

Del. Eleanor Holmes Norton (D-AL)
2136 Rayburn House Office Building
(202) 225-8050; 225-3002
Washington: (202) 783-5065
Web Site

Florida

Rep. Jeff Miller (R-1st)
336 Cannon House Office Building
(202) 225-4136; 225-3414
Pensacola: (850) 479-1183
Web Site

Rep. Steve Southerland (R-2nd)
1229 Longworth House Office Building
(202) 225-5235; 225-5615
Panama City: (850) 785-0812
Web Site

Rep. Tedd Yoho (R-3rd) **
511 Cannon House Office Building
(202) 225-5744; 225-2256
Gainsville: N/A
Web Site

Rep. Ander Crenshaw (R-4th)
440 Cannon House Office Building
(202) 225-2501; 225-2504
Jacksonville: (904) 598-0481
Web Site

Rep. Corrine Brown (D-5th)
2111 Rayburn House Office Building
(202) 225-0123; 225-2256
Jacksonville: (904) 354-1652
Web Site

Rep. Ron DeSantis (R-6th) **
427 Cannon House Office Building
(202) 225-2706; 225-3973
Port Orange: (386) 756-9798
Web Site

Rep. John Mica (R-7th)
2187 Rayburn House Office Building
(202) 225-4035; 226-0821
Maitland: (407) 657-8080
Web Site

Rep. Bill Posey (R-8th)
120 Cannon House Office Building
(202) 225-3671; 225-3516
Melbourne: (407) 632-1776
Web Site

Florida cont.

Rep. Alan Grayson (D-9th) **
430 Cannon House Office Building
(202) 225-9889; 225-4085
Palm Harbor?: N/A
Web Site

Rep. Daniel Webster (R-10th)
1039 Longworth House Office Building
(202) 225-2176; 225-0999
Winter Garden: (407) 654-5705
Web Site

Rep. Richard Nugent (R-11th)
1727 Longworth House Office Building
(202) 225-1002; 226-6559
Brooksville: (352) 799-8354
Web Site

Rep. Gus M. Bilirakis (R-12th)
2313 Rayburn House Office Building
(202) 225-5755; 225-4085
Tarpon Springs: (727) 940-5860

Rep. Bill Young (R-13th)
2407 Rayburn House Office Building
(202) 225-5961; 225-9764
St. Petersburg: (813) 893-3191
Web Site

Rep. Kathy Castor (D-14th)
205 Cannon House Office Building
(202) 225-3376; 225-5652
Tampa: (813) 871-2817
Web Site

Rep. Dennis Ross (R-15th)
229 Cannon House Offcie Building
(202) 225-1252; 226-0585
Lakeland: (863) 644-8215
Web Site

Rep. Vern Buchanan (R-16th)
2104 Rayburn House Office Building
(202) 225-5015; 226-0828
Sarasota: (941) 951-6643
Web Site

Florida cont.

Rep. Tom Rooney (R-17th)
221 Cannon House Office Building
(202) 225-5792; 225-3132
Punta Gorda: (941) 575-9101
Web Site

Rep. Patrick Murphy (D-18th) **
1517 Longworth House Office Building
(202) 225-3026; 225-8398
Palm Beach Gardens: (561) 253-8433
Web Site

Rep. Trey Radel (R-19th) **
1123 Longworth House Office Building
(202) 225-2536; 225-5974
Cape Coral: N/A
Web Site

Rep. Alcee Hastings (D-20th)
2353 Rayburn House Office Building
(202) 225-1313; 225-1171
Ft. Lauderdale: (954) 733-2800
Web Site

Rep. Ted Deutch (R-21st)
1024 Longworth House Office Building
(202) 225-3001; 225-5974
Boca Raton: (561) 470-5440
Web Site

Rep. Lois Frankel (D-22nd) **
1037 Longworth House Office Building
(202) 225-9890; 225-8398
Boca Raton: (561) 998-9045
Web Site

Rep. Debbie Wasserman Schultz (D-23)
118 Cannon House Office Building
(202) 225-7931; 226-2052
Pembroke Pines: (954) 437-3936
Web Site

Rep. Frederica Wilson (D-24th)
208 Cannon House Offcie Building
(202) 225-4506; 226-0777
Miami Gardens: (305) 690-5905
Web Site

Florida cont.

Rep. Mario Diaz-Balart (R-25th)
436 Cannon House Office Building
(202) 225-4211; 225-8576
Miami: (305) 225-6866
Web Site

Rep. Joe Garcia (D-26th) **
1440 Cannon House Office Building
(202) 225-2778; 226-0346
Miami: N/A
Web Site

Rep. Ileana Ros-Lehtinen (R-27th)
2206 Rayburn House Office Building
(202) 225-3931; 225-5620
Miami: (305) 668-2285
Web Site

Georgia

Rep. Jack Kingston (R-1st)
2372 Rayburn House Office Building
(202) 225-5831; 226-2269
Savannah: (912) 352-0101
Web Site

Rep. Sanford Bishop, Jr. (D-2nd)
2429 Rayburn House Office Building
(202) 225-3631; 225-2203
Albany: (912) 439-8067
Web Site

Rep. Lynn Westmoreland (R-3rd)
2433 Rayburn House Office Building
(202) 225-5901; 225-2515
Newnan: (770) 683-2033
Web Site

Rep. Hank Johnson (D-4th)
1427 Longworth House Office Building
(202) 225-1605; 226-0691
Lithonia: (770) 987-2291
Web Site

Rep. John Lewis (D-5th)
343 Cannon House Office Building
(202) 225-3801; 225-0351
Atlanta: (404) 659-0116

Georgia cont.

Rep. Tom Price (R-6th)
403 Cannon House Office Building
(202) 225-4501; 225-4656
Marietta: (770) 565-4990
Web Site

Rep. Rob Woodall (R-7th)
1725 Longworth House Office Building
(202) 225-4272; 225-4696
Lawrenceville: (770) 232-3005
Web Site

Rep. Austin Scott (D-8th)
516 Cannon House Office Building
(202) 225-6531; 225-3013
Warner Robins: (478) 971-1776
Web Site

Rep. Doug Collins (R-9th) **
513 Cannon House Office Building
(202) 225-9893; N/A
Gainsville: N/A
Web Site

Rep. Paul Broun (R-10th)
325 Cannon House Office Building
(202) 225-4101; 226-0776
Evans: (706) 447-3857
Web Site

Rep. Phil Gingrey (R-11th)
442 Cannon House Office Building
(202) 225-2931; 225-2944
Marietta: (770) 429-1776
Web Site

Rep. John Barrow (D-12th)
2202 Rayburn House Office Building
(202) 225-2823; 225-3377
Augusta: (706) 722-4494
Web Site

Rep. David Scott (D-13th)
225 Cannon House Office Building
(202) 225-2939; 225-4628
Jonesboro: (770) 210-5073
Web Site

Georgia cont.

Rep. Tom Graves (R-14th)
1113 Longworth House Office Building
(202) 225-5211; 225-8272
Dalton: 706-226-5320
Web Site

Guam

Del. Madeleine Bordallo (D-AL)
2441 Rayburn House Office Building
(202) 225-1118; 226-0341
Hagatna: (671) 477-4272
Web Site

Hawaii

Rep. Colleen Hanabusa (D-1st)
238 Cannon House Office Building
(202) 225-2726; 225-4580
Honolulu: (808) 541-2570
Web Site

Rep. Tulsi Gabbard (D-2nd) **
502 Cannon House Office Building
(202) 225-4906; 225-4987
Honolulu: N/A
Web Site

Idaho

Rep. Raul Labrador (R-1st)
1523 Longworth House Office Building
(202) 225-6611; 225-3029
Meridan: (208) 888-3188
Web Site

Rep. Mike Simpson (R-2nd)
2312 Rayburn House Office Building
(202) 225-5531; 225-8216
Boise: (208) 334-1953
Web Site

Illinois

Rep. Bobby Rush (D-1st)
2268 Rayburn House Office Building
(202) 225-4372; 226-0333
Chicago: (773) 224-6500
Web Site

Rep. VACANT (-2nd) **
Special Election April 9, 2013
2419 Rayburn House Office Building
(202) 225-0773; 225-0899
Chicago: (773) 734-9660
Web Site

Rep. Dan Lipinski (D-3rd)
1717 Longworth House Office Building
(202) 225-5701; 225-1012
Chicago: (312) 886-0481
Web Site

Rep. Luiz Gutierrez (D-4th)
2266 Rayburn House Office Building
(202) 225-8203; 225-7810
Chicago: (773) 342-0774
Web Site

Rep. Mike Quigley (D-5th)
1124 Longworth House Office Building
(202) 225-4061; 225-5603
Chicago: (773) 267-5926
Web Site

Rep. Peter Roskam (R-6th)
227 Cannon House Office Building
(202) 225-4561; 225-1166
Bloomingdale: (630) 893-9670
Web Site

Rep. Danny Davis (D-7th)
2159 Rayburn House Office Building
(202) 225-5006; 225-5641
Chicago: (773) 533-7520
Web Site

Rep. Tammy Duckworth (D-8th) **
108 Cannon House Office Building
(202) 225-3711; 225-7830
Schaumburg: N/A
Web Site

Illinois cont.

Rep. Jan Schakowsky (D-9th)
2367 Rayburn House Office Building
(202) 225-2111; 226-6890
Chicago: (773) 506-7100
Web Site

Rep. Brad Schneider (D-10th) **
317 Cannon House Office Building
(202) 225-4835; 225-0837
Lincolnshire: (847) 793-0625
Web Site

Rep. Bill Foster (D-11th) **
2113 Rayburn House Office Building
(202) 225-3515; 225-9420
N/A
Web Site

Rep. William Enyart (D-12th) **
1722 Longworth House Office Building
(202) 225-5661; 225-0285
Belleville: (618) 233-8026
Web Site

Rep. Rodney Davis (R-13th) **
1740 Longworth House Office Building
(202) 225-2371; 226-0791
Champaign: (217) 403-4690
Web Site

Rep. Randy Hultgren (R-14th)
332 Cannon House Office Building
(202) 225-2976; 225-0697
Geneva: (630) 232-7104
Web Site

Rep. John Shimkus (R-15th)
2452 Rayburn House Office Building
(202) 225-5271; 225-5880
Springfield: (217) 492-5090
Web Site

Rep. Adam Kinzinger (R-16th)
1221 Longworth House Office Building
(202) 225-3635; 225-3521
Joliet: (815) 726-4998
Web Site

Illinois cont.

Rep. Cheri Bustos (D-17th) **
1009 Longworth House Office Building
(202) 225-5905; 225-5396
Rock Island: (309) 786-3406
Web Site

Rep. Aaron Schock (R-18th)
328 Cannon House Office Building
(202) 225-6201; 225-9249
Peoria: (309) 671-7027
Web Site

Indiana

Rep. Peter Visclosky (D-1st)
2256 Rayburn House Office Building
(202) 225-2461; 225-2493
Merrillville: (219) 795-1844
Web Site

Rep. Jackie Walorski (R-2nd) **
419 Cannon House Office Building
(202) 225-3915; 225-6798
Mishawaka: (574) 204-2645
Web Site

Rep. Marlin Stutzman (R-3rd)
1728 Longworth House Office Building
(202) 225-4436; 226-9870
Winona Lake: (574) 269-1940
Web Site

Rep. Todd Rokita (R-4th)
236 Cannon House Office Building
(202) 225-5037;226-0544
Plainfield: (317) 838-0404
Web Site

Rep. Susan Brooks (R-5th) **
1505 Longworth House Office Building
(202) 225-2276; 225-0016
Indianapolis: (317) 848-0201

Indiana cont.

Rep. Luke Messer (R-6th) **
508 Cannon House Office Building
(202) 225-3021; 225-3382
Muncie: (765) 747-5566
Web Site

Rep. Andre Carson (D-7th)
425 Cannon House Office Building
(202) 225-4011; 225-5633
Indianapolis: (317) 283-6516
Web Site

Rep. Larry Bucshon (R-8th)
1123 Longworth House Office Building
(202) 225-4636; 225-3284
Evansville: (812) 465-6484
Web Site

Rep. Todd Young (R-9th)
1721 Longworth House Office Building
(202) 225-5315; 226-6866
Jeffersonville: (812) 288-3999
Web Site

Iowa

Rep. Bruce Braley (D-1st)
1727 Longworth House Office Building
(202) 225-2911; 225-6666
Waterloo: (319) 287-3233
Web Site

Rep. Dave Loebsack (D-2nd)
1527 Longworth House Office Building
(202) 225-6576; 226-0757
Iowa City: (319) 351-0789
Web Site

Rep. Tom Latham (R-3rd)
2217 Rayburn House Office Building
(202) 225-5476; 225-3301
Ames: (515) 232-2885
Web Site

Iowa cont.

Rep. Steve King (R-4th)
1131 Longworth House Office Building
(202) 225-4426; 225-3193
Storm Lake: (712) 732-4197
Web Site

Kansas

Rep. Tim Huelskamp (R-1st)
126 Cannon House Office Building
(202) 225-2715; 225-5124
Hutchinson: (620) 665-6138
Web Site

Rep. Lynn Jenkins (R-2nd)
1122 Longworth House Office Building
(202) 225-6601; 225-7986
Topeka: (785) 234-5966
Web Site

Rep. Kevin Yoder (R-3rd)
214 Cannon House Office Building
(202) 225-2865; 225-2807
Kansas City: (913) 621-0832
Web Site

Rep. Mike Pompeo (R-4th)
107 Cannon House Office Building
(202) 225-6216; 225-3489
Wichita: (316) 262-8992
Web Site

Kentucky

Rep. Edward Whitfield (R-1st)
2368 Rayburn House Office Building
(202) 225-3115; 225-3547
Hopkinsville: (502) 885-8079
Web Site

Rep. Brett Guthrie (R-2nd)
308 Cannon House Office Building
(202) 225-3501; 226-2019
Bowling Green: (270) 842-9896
Web Site

Kansas cont.

Rep. John Yarmuth (D-3rd)
435 Cannon House Office Building
(202) 225-5401; 225-5776
Louisville: (502) 582-5129
Web Site

Rep. Thomas Massie (R-4th) **
314 Cannon House Office Building
(202) 225-3465; 225-0003
Ft. Mitchell: (859) 426-0080
Web Site

Rep. Harold Rogers (R-5th)
2406 Rayburn House Office Building
(202) 225-4601; 225-0940
Somerset: (606) 679-8346
Web Site

Rep. Garland Barr, IV (R-6th) **
1432 Longworth House Office Building
(202) 225-4706; 225-2122
Lexington: (859) 219-1366
Web Site

Louisiana

Rep. Steve Scalise (R-1st)
429 Cannon House Office Building
Metairie: (504) 837-1259
Web Site

Rep. Cedric Richmond (D-2nd)
415 Cannon House Office Building
(202) 225-6636; 225-1988
New Orleans: (504) 288-3777
Web Site

Rep. Charles Boustany, Jr. (R-3rd)
1431 Longworth House Office Building
(202) 225-2031; 225-5724
Lafayette: (337) 235-6322
Web Site

Louisiana cont.

Rep. John Fleming (R-4th)
416 Cannon House Office Building
(202) 225-2777; 225-8039
Shreveport: (318) 798-2254
Web Site

Rep. Rodney Alexander (D-5th)
316 Cannon House Office Building
(202) 225-8490; 225-5639
Alexandria: (318) 445-0818
Web Site

Rep. Bill Cassidy (R-6th)
1535 Longworth House Office Building
(202) 225-3901; 225-7313
Baton Rouge: (504) 929-7711
Web Site

Maine

Rep. Chellie Pingree (D-1st)
1318 Longworth House Office Building
(202) 225-6116; 225-5590
Portland: (207) 774-5019
Web Site

Rep. Michael Michaud (D-2nd)
1724 Longworth House Office Building
(202) 225-6306; 225-2943
Bangor: (207) 942-6935
Web Site

Maryland

Rep. Andy Harris (R-1st)
506 Cannon House Office Building
(202) 225-5311; 225-0254
Salisbury: (443) 944-8624
Web Site

Rep. Dutch Ruppersberger (D-2nd)
2453 Rayburn House Office Building
(202) 225-3061; 225-3094
Timonium: (410) 628-2701
Web Site

Maryland cont.

Rep. John Sarbanes (D-3rd)
2444 Rayburn House Office Building
(202) 225-4016; 225-9219
Towson: (410) 832-8890
Web Site

Rep. Donna Edwards (D-4th)
318 Cannon House Office Building
(202) 225-8699; 225-8714
Silver Spring: (301) 562-7960
Web Site

Rep. Steny Hoyer (D-5th)
1705 Longworth House Office Building
(202) 225-4131; 225-4300
Greenbelt: (301) 474-0119
Web Site

Rep. John Delaney (D-6th) **
1632 Longworth House Office Building
(202) 225-2721; 225-2193
Gaithersburg: (301) 926-0300
Web Site

Rep. Elijah Cummings (D-7th)
2235 Rayburn House Office Building
(202) 225-4741; 225-3178
Baltimore: (410) 685-9199
Web Site

Rep. Chris Van Hollen, Jr. (D-8th)
1707 Longworth House Office Building
(202) 225-5341; 225-0375
Rockville: (301) 424-3501
Web Site

Massachusetts

Rep. Richard Neal (D-1st)
2208 Rayburn House Office Building
(202) 225-5601; 225-8112
Springfield: (413) 785-0325
Web Site

Massachusetts cont.

Rep. James McGovern (D-2nd)
4380 Cannon House Office Building
(202) 225-6101; 225-5759
Worcester: (508) 831-7356
Web Site

Rep. Niki Tsongas (D-3rd)
1607 Longworth House Office Building
(202) 225-3411; 226-0771
Lowell: (978) 459-0101
Web Site

Rep. Joseph P. Kennedy, III (D-4th) **
1218 Longworth House Office Building
(202) 225-5931; 225-0182
Newton: (617) 332-3333
Web Site

Rep. Edward Markey (D-5th)
2108 Rayburn House Office Building
(202) 225-2836; 226-0092
Medford: (781) 396-2900
Web Site

Rep. John Tierney (D-6th)
2238 Rayburn House Office Building
(202) 225-8020; 225-5915
Peabody: (978) 531-1669
Web Site

Rep. Michael Capuano (D-7th)
1414 Longworth House Office Building
(202) 225-5111; 225-9322
Cambridge: (617) 621-6208
Web Site

Rep. Stephen Lynch (D-8th)
2348 Rayburn House Office Building
(202) 225-8273; 225-3984
Boston: (617) 428-2000
Web Site

Rep. Bill Keating (D-9th)
315 Cannon House Office Building
(202) 225-3111; 225-5658
Quincy: (617) 770-3700
Web Site

Michigan

Rep. Dan Benishek (R-1st)
514 Cannon House Office Building
(202) 225-4735; 225-4710
Marquette: 906-273-1661
Web Site

Rep. Bill Huizenga (R-2nd)
1217 Longworth House Office Building
(202) 225-4401; 226-0779
Holland: (616) 395-0030
Web Site

Rep. Justin Amash (R-3rd)
114 Cannon House Office Building
(202) 225-3831; 225-5144
Grand Rapids: (616) 451-8383
Web Site

Rep. Dave Camp (R-4th)
341 Cannon House Office Building
(202) 225-3561; 225-9679
Midland: (989) 631-2552
Web Site

Rep. Dale Kildee (D-5th)
2107 Rayburn House Office Building
(202) 225-3611; 225-6393
Flint: (810) 239-1437
Web Site

Rep. Fred Upton (R-6th)
2183 Rayburn House Office Building
(202) 225-3761; 225-4986
Kalamazoo: (616) 385-0039
Web Site

Rep. Tim Walberg (R-7th)
418 Cannon House Office Building
(202) 225-6276; 225-6281
Jackson: (517) 780-9075
Web Site

Rep. Mike Rogers (R-8th)
133 Cannon House Office Building
(202) 225-4872; 225-5820
Lansing: (877) 333-6453
Web Site

Michigan cont.

Rep. Sandy Levin (D-9th)
1236 Longworth House Office Building
(202) 225-4961; 226-1033
Roseville: (586) 498-7122
Web Site

Rep. Candice Miller (R-10th)
1034 Longworth House Office Building
(202) 225-2106; 226-1169
Shelby Township: (586) 997-5010
Web Site

Rep. Kerry Bentivolio (R-11th) **
226 Cannon House Office Building
(202) 225-8171; 225-2667
Commerce: (248) 859-2982
Web Site

Rep. John Dingell (D-12th)
2328 Rayburn House Office Building
(202) 225-4071; 226-0371
Dearborn: (313) 278-2936
Web Site

Rep. John Conyers (D-13th)
2426 Rayburn House Office Building
(202) 225-5126; 225-0072
Detroit: (313) 961-5670
Web Site

Rep. Gary Peters (D-14th)
1609 Longworth House Office Building
(202) 225-5802; 226-2356
Troy: (248) 273-4227

Minnesota

Rep. Tim Walz (D-1st)
1722 Longworth House Office Building
(202) 225-2472; 225-3433
Mankato: (507) 388-2149
Web Site

Rep. John Kline (R-2nd)
2439 Rayburn House Office Building
(202) 225-2271; 225-2595
Burnsville: (952) 808-1213

Minnesota cont.

Rep. Erik Paulsen (R-3rd)
127 Cannon House Office Building
(202) 225-2871; 225-6351
Minnetonka: (952) 405-8510
Web Site

Rep. Betty McCollum (D-4th)
1714 Longworth House Office Building
(202) 225-6631; 225-1968
St. Paul: (612) 224-9191
Web Site

Rep. Keith Ellison (D-5th)
1027 Longworth House Office Building
(202) 225-4755; 225-4886
Minneapolis: (612) 522-1212
Web Site

Rep. Michele Bachmann (R-6th)
103 Cannon House Office Building
(202) 225-2331; 225-6475
Woodbury: (651) 731-5400
Web Site

Rep. Collin Peterson (D-7th)
2211 Rayburn House Office Building
(202) 225-2165; 225-1593
Detroit Lakes: (218) 847-5056
Web Site

Rep. Rick Nolan (D-8th) **
2447 Rayburn House Office Building
(202) 225-6211; 225-0699
Brainerd: (218) 545-4078
Web Site

Mississippi

Rep. Alan Nunnelee (R-1st)
1432 Longworth House Office Building
(202) 225-4306; 225-3549
Tupelo: (662) 841-8808

Mississippi cont.

Rep. Bennie Thompson (D-2nd)
2466 Rayburn House Office Building
(202) 225-5876; 225-5898
Bolton: (800) 355-9003
Web Site

Rep. Gregg Harper (R-3rd)
307 Cannon House Office Building
(202) 225-5031; 225-5797
Pearl: (601) 932-2410
Web Site

Rep. Steven Palazzo (R-4th)
331 Cannon House Office Building
(202) 225-5772; 225-7074
Gulfport: (228) 864-7670
Web Site

Missouri

Rep. William Lacy Clay, Jr. (D-1st)
2418 Rayburn House Office Building
(202) 225-2406; 226-3717
St. Louis: (314) 367-1970
Web Site

Rep. Ann Wagner (R-2nd) **
435 Cannon House Office Building
(202) 225-1621; 225-2563
Ballwin: (636) 779-5449
Web Site

Rep. Blaine Luetkemeyer (R-3rd)
1740 Longworth House Office Building
(202) 225-2956; 225-5712
Columbia: (573) 443-1041
Web Site

Rep. Vicky Hartzler (R-4th)
1023 Longworth House Office Building
(202) 225-2876; 225-0148
Jefferson City: (573) 634-4884
Web Site

Missouri cont.

Rep. Emanuel Cleaver, II (D-5th)
1433 Longworth House Office Building
(202) 225-4535; 225-4403
Kansas City: (816) 842-4545
Web Site

Rep. Sam Graves (R-6th)
1415 Longworth House Office Building
(202) 225-7041; 225-8221
Liberty: (816) 792-3976
Web Site

Rep. Billy Long (R-7th)
1541 Longworth House Office Building
(202) 225-6536; 225-5604
Springfield: (417) 889-1800
Web Site

Rep. Jo Ann Emerson (R-8th)
2230 Rayburn House Office Building
(202) 225-4404; 226-0326
Cape Girardeau: (573) 335-0101
Web Site

Montana

Rep. Steve Daines (R-AL) **
206 Cannon House Office Building
(202) 225-3211; 225-5687
Billings: (406) 969-1736
Web Site

Nebraska

Rep. Jeff Fortenberry (R-1st)
1514 Longworth House Office Building
(202) 225-4806; 225-5686
Lincoln: (402) 438-1598
Web Site

Rep. Lee Terry (R-2nd)
2331 Rayburn House Office Building
(202) 225-4155; 226-5452
Omaha: (402) 397-9944

Nebraska cont.

Rep. Adrian Smith (R-3rd)
503 Cannon House Office Building
(202) 225-6435; 225-0207
Scottsbluff: (308) 633-3333
Web Site

Nevada

Rep. Dina Titus (D-1st) **
401 Cannon House Office Building
(202) 225-5965; 225-3119
Las Vegas: (702) 220-9823
Web Site

Rep. Mark Amodei (R-2nd)
125 Cannon House Office Building
(202) 225-6155; 225-5679
Reno: (775) 686-5760
Web Site

Rep. Joe Heck (R-3rd)
132 Cannon House Office Building
(202) 225-3252; 225-2185
Las Vegas: (702) 387-4941
Web Site

Rep. Steven Horsford (D-4th) **
1330 Longworth House Office Building
(202) 225-9894; 225-9783
N. Las Vegas: (702) 802-4500
Web Site

New Hampshire

Rep. Carol Shea-Porter (D-1st) **
1530 Longworth House Office Building
(202) 225-5456; 225-5822
Manchester: (603) 641-9536
Web Site

Rep. Ann McLane Kuster (D-2nd) **
137 Cannon House Office Building
(202) 225-5206; 225-2946
Concord (603) 226-1002

New Jersey

Rep. Robert Andrews (D-1st)
2265 Rayburn House Office Building
(202) 225-6501; 225-6583
Haddon Heights: (856) 546-5100
Web Site

Rep. Frank LoBiondo (R-2nd)
2427 Rayburn House Office Building
(202) 225-6572; 225-3318
Mays Landing: (800) 471-4450
Web Site

Rep. Jon Runyan (R-3rd)
1239 Longworth House Office Building
(202) 225-4765; 225-0778
Mount Laurel: (856) 780-6436
Web Site

Rep. Christopher Smith (R-4th)
2373 Rayburn House Office Building
(202) 225-3765; 225-7768
Hamilton: (609) 585-7878
Web Site

Rep. Scott Garrett (R-5th)
2244 Rayburn House Office Building
(202) 225-4465; 225-9048
Newton: (973) 300-2000
Web Site

Rep. Frank Pallone, Jr. (D-6th)
237 Cannon House Office Building
(202) 225-4671; 225-9665
Long Branch: (732) 571-1140
Web Site

Rep. Leonard Lance (R-7th)
426 Cannon House Office Building
(202) 225-5361; 225-9460
Westfield: (908) 518-7733
Web Site

Rep. Albio Sires (D-8th)
2342 Rayburn House Office Building
(202) 225-7919; 226-0792
Jersey City: (201) 222-2828
Web Site

New Jersey cont.

Rep. Bill Pascrell, Jr. (D-9th)
2370 Rayburn House Office Building
(202) 225-5751; 225-5782
Paterson: (973) 523-5152
Web Site

Rep. Donald Payne (D-10th)
2310 Rayburn House Office Building
(202) 225-3436; 225-4160
Newark: (973) 645-3213
Web Site

Rep. Rodney Frelinghuysen (R-11th)
2369 Rayburn House Office Building
(202) 225-5034; 225-3186
Morristown: (973) 984-0711
Web Site

Rep. Rush Holt (D-12th)
1214 Longworth House Office Building
(202) 225-5801; 225-6025
West Windsor: (609) 750-9365
Web Site

New Mexico

Rep. Lujan Grisham (D-1st) **
214 Cannon House Office Building
(202) 225-6316; 225-4975
Albuquerque: (505) 346-6781
Web Site

Rep. Steve Pearce (R-2nd)
2432 Rayburn House Office Building
(202) 225-2365; 225-9599
Las Cruces: (855) 473-2723
Web Site

Rep. Ben R. Lujan (D-3rd)
502 Cannon House Office Building
(202) 225-6190; 226-1528
Santa Fe: (505) 984-8950
Web Site

New York

Rep. Tim Bishop (D-1st)
306 Cannon House Office Building
(202) 225-3826; 225-3143
Coram: (631) 696-6500
Web Site

Rep. Peter King (R-2nd)
339 Cannon House Office Building
(202) 225-7896; 226-2279
Massapequa Park: (516) 541-4225
Web Site

Rep. Steve Israel (D-3rd)
2457 Rayburn House Office Building
(202) 225-3335; 225-4669
Hauppauge: (631) 951-2210
Web Site

Rep. Carolyn McCarthy (D-4th)
2346 Rayburn House Office Building
(202) 225-5516; 225-5758
Garden City: (516) 739-3008
Web Site

Rep. Gregory Meeks (D-5th)
2234 Rayburn House Office Building
(202) 225-3461; 226-4169
Far Rockaway: (718) 327-9791
Web Site

Rep. Grace Meng (D-6th) **
1317 Longworth House Office Building
(202) 225-2601; 225-1598
Bayside: (718) 423-2154
Web Site

Rep. Nydia Velazquez (D-7th)
2302 Rayburn House Office Building
(202) 225-2361; 226-0327
Brooklyn: (718) 599-3658
Web Site

Rep. Hakeem Jeffries (D-8th) **
1339 Longworth House Office Building
(202) 225-5936; 225-1018
Brooklyn: (718) 373-0033
Web Site

New York cont.

Rep. Yvette Clarke (D-9th)
1029 Longworth House Office Building
(202) 225-6231; 226-0112
Brooklyn: (718) 287-1142
Web Site

Rep. Jerrold Nadler (D-10th)
2334 Rayburn House Office Building
(202) 225-5635; 225-6923
New York: (212) 367-7350
Web Site

Rep. Mike Grimm (R-11th)
521 Cannon House Office Building
(202) 225-3371; 226-1272
Staten Island: (718) 351-1062
Web Site

Rep. Carolyn Maloney (D-12th)
2332 Rayburn House Office Building
(202) 225-7944; 225-4709
New York: (212) 860-0606
Web Site

Rep. Charles Rangel (D-13th)
2354 Rayburn House Office Building
(202) 225-4365; 225-0816
New York: (212) 663-3900
Web Site

Rep. Joseph Crowley (D-14th)
2404 Rayburn House Office Building
(202) 225-3965; 225-1909
Jackson Heights: (718) 779-1400
Web Site

Rep. Jose Serrano (D-15th)
2227 Rayburn House Office Building
(202) 225-4361; 225-6001
Bronx: (718) 620-0084
Web Site

Rep. Eliot Engel (D-16th)
2161 Rayburn House Office Building
(202) 225-2464; 225-5513
Bronx: (718) 796-9700
Web Site

New York cont.

Rep. Nita Lowey (D-17th)
2365 Rayburn House Office Building
(202) 225-6506; 225-0546
White Plains: (914) 428-1707
Web Site

Rep. Sean Patrick Maloney (D-18th) **
1529 Longworth House Office Building
(202) 225-5441; 225-3289
Fishkill: (845) 202-0563
Web Site

Rep. Christopher Gibson (R-19th)
502 Cannon House Office Building
(202) 225-5614; 225-1168
Glens Falls: (518) 743-0964
Web Site

Rep. Paul Tonko (D-20th)
422 Cannon House Office Building
(202) 225-5076; 225-5077
Albany: (518) 465-0700
Web Site

Rep. Bill Owens (D-21st)
431 Cannon House Office Building
(202) 225-4611; 226-0621
Watertown: (315) 782-3150
Web Site

Rep. Richard Hanna (R-22nd)
319 Cannon House Office Building
(202) 225-3665; 225-1891
Utica: (315) 724-9740
Web Site

Rep. Thomas Reed (R-23rd)
1037 Longworth House Office Building
(202) 225-3161; 226-6599
Pittsford: 585-218-0040
Web Site

Rep. Daniel Maffei (D-24th) **
422 Cannon House Office Building
(202) 225-3701; 225-4042
Auburn: N/A
Web Site

New York cont.

Rep. Louise Slaughter (D-25th)
2469 Rayburn House Office Building
(202) 225-3615; 225-7822
Rochester: (716) 232-4850
Web Site

Rep. Brian Higgins (D-26th)
2459 Rayburn House Office Building
(202) 225-3306; 226-0347
Buffalo: (716) 852-3501
Web Site

Rep. Chris Collins (R-27th) **
1711 Longworth House Office Building
(202) 225-5265; 225-5910
Williamsville: (716) 634-2324
Web Site

North Carolina

Rep. G. K. Butterfield (D-1st)
2305 Rayburn House Office Building
(202) 225-3101; 225-3354
Weldon: (252) 538-4123
Web Site

Rep. Renee Ellmers (R-2nd)
1533 Longworth House Office Building
(202) 225-4531; 225-5662
Dunn: (910) 230-1910
Web Site

Rep. Walter Jones (R-3rd)
2333 Rayburn House Office Building
(202) 225-3415; 225-3286
Greenville: (800) 351-1697
Web Site

Rep. David Price (D-4th)
2162 Rayburn House Office Building
(202) 225-1784; 225-2014
Raleigh: (919) 859-5999
Web Site

North Carolina cont.

Rep. Virginia Foxx (R-5th)
1230 Longworth House Office Building
(202) 225-2071; 225-2995
Clemmons: (336) 778-0211
Web Site

Rep. Howard Coble (R-6th)
2118 Rayburn House Office Building
(202) 225-3065; 225-8611
Greensboro: (336) 333-5005
Web Site

Rep. Mike McIntyre (D-7th)
2133 Rayburn House Office Building
(202) 225-2731; 225-5773
Fayetteville: (910) 323-0260
Web Site

Rep. Richard Hudson (D-8th) **
429 Cannon House Office Building
(202) 225-3715; 225-4036
Concord: (704) 786-1612
Web Site

Rep. Robert Pittenger (R-9th) **
224 Cannon House Office Building
(202) 225-1976; 225-3389
Charlotte: (704) 365-6234
Web Site

Rep. Patrick McHenry (R-10th)
224 Cannon House Office Building
(202) 225-2576; 225-0316
Hickory: (828) 327-6100
Web Site

Rep. Mark Meadows (R-11th) **
1516 Longworth House Office Building
(202) 225-6401; 226-6422
Hendersonville: (828) 693-5660
Web Site

Rep. Melvin Watt (D-12th)
2304 Rayburn House Office Building
(202) 225-1510; 225-1512
Charlotte: (704) 344-9950
Web Site

North Carolina cont.

Rep. George Holding (R-13th) **
507 Cannon House Office Building
(202) 225-3032; 225-0181
Raleigh: (919) 856-9778
Web Site

North Dakota

Rep. Kevin Cramer (R-AL) **
1032 Longworth House Office Building
(202) 225-2611; 226-0893
Bismarck: N/A
Web Site

Ohio

Rep. Steve Chabot (R-1st)
2351 Rayburn House Office Building
(202) 225-2216; 225-3012
Cincinnati: (513) 684-2723
Web Site

Rep. Brad Wenstrup (R-2nd) **
1223 Longworth House Office Building
(202) 225-3164; 225-1992
Cincinnati: (513) 474-7777
Web Site

Rep. Joyce Beatty (D-3rd) **
417 Cannon House Office Building
(202) 225-6465; 225-6754
Columbus: (614) 220-0003
Web Site

Rep. Jim Jordan (R-4th)
1524 Longworth House Office Building
(202) 225-2676; 226-0577
Mansfield: (419) 522-5757
Web Site

Rep. Robert Latta (R-5th)
1323 Longworth House Office Building
(202) 225-6405; 225-1985
Norwalk: (419) 668-0206
Web Site

Ohio cont.

Rep. Bill Johnson (R-6th)
317 Cannon House Office Building
(202) 225-5705; 225-5907
Marietta: (740) 376-0868
Web Site

Rep. Bob Gibbs (R-7th)
329 Cannon House Office Building
(202) 225-6265; 225-3394
Zanesville: (740) 452-2279
Web Site

Rep. John Boehner (R-8th)
1011 Longworth House Office Building
(202) 225-6205; 225-0704
West Chester: (513) 779-5400
Web Site

Rep. Marcy Kaptur (D-9th)
2186 Rayburn House Office Building
(202) 225-4146; 225-7711
Toledo: (419) 259-7500
Web Site

Rep. Michael Turner (R-10th)
2454 Rayburn House Office Building
(202) 225-6465; 225-6754
Dayton: (937) 225-2843
Web Site

Rep. Marcia Fudge (D-11th)
1019 Longworth House Office Building
(202) 225-7032; 225-1339
Warrensville: (216) 522-4900
Web Site

Rep. Patrick Tiberi (R-12th)
106 Cannon House Office Building
(202) 225-5355; 226-4523
Columbus: (614) 523-2555
Web Site

Rep. Tim Ryan (D-13th)
1421 Longworth House Office Building
(202) 225-5261; 225-3719
Youngstown: (330) 740-0193
Web Site

Ohio cont.

Rep. David Joyce (R-14th) **
1535 Longworth House Office Building
(202) 225-5731; 225-3307
Painesville: (440) 352-3939
Web Site

Rep. Steve Stivers (R-15th)
1007 Longworth House Office Building
(202) 225-2015; 225-3529
Columbus: (614) 299-6415
Web Site

Rep. Jim Renacci (R-16th)
130 Cannon House Office Building
(202) 225-3876; 225-3059
Canton: 330-489-4414
Web Site

Oklahoma

Rep. Jim Bridenstine (R-1st) **
216 Cannon House Office Building
(202) 225-2211; 225-9187
Tulsa: (918) 935-3222
Web Site

Rep. Markwayne Mullin (R-2nd) **
1113 Longworth House Office Building
(202) 225-2701; 225-3038
Claremore: (918) 341-9336
Web Site

Rep. Frank Lucas (R-3rd)
2311 Rayburn House Office Building
(202) 225-5565; 225-8698
Yukon: (405) 373-1958
Web Site

Rep. Tom Cole (R-4th)
2458 Rayburn House Office Building
(202) 225-6165; 225-3512
Norman: (405) 329-6500
Web Site

Oklahoma cont.

Rep. James Lankford (R-5th)
509 Cannon House Office Building
(202) 225-2132; 226-1463
Oklahoma City: (405) 234-9900
Web Site

Oregon

Rep. Suzanne Bonamici (D-1st)
2338 Rayburn House Office Building
(202) 225-0855; 225-9497
Portland: (800) 422-4003
Web Site

Rep. Greg Walden (R-2nd)
2182 Rayburn House Office Building
(202) 225-6730; 225-5774
Medford: (800) 533-3303
Web Site

Rep. Earl Blumenauer (D-3rd)
1502 Longworth House Office Building
(202) 225-4811; 225-8941
Portland: (503) 231-2300
Web Site

Rep. Peter DeFazio (D-4th)
2134 Rayburn House Office Building
(202) 225-6416; 226-3493
Eugene: (541) 465-6732
Web Site

Rep. Kurt Schrader (D-5th)
314 Cannon House Office Building
(202) 225-5711; 225-5699
Salem: (503) 588-9100
Web Site

Pennsylvania

Rep. Robert Brady (D-1st)
102 Cannon House Office Building
(202) 225-4731; 225-0088
Philadelphia: (215) 389-4627

Pennsylvania cont.

Rep. Chaka Fattah (D-2nd)
2301 Rayburn House Office Building
(202) 225-4001; 225-5392
Philadelphia: (215) 387-6404
Web Site

Rep. Mike Kelly (R-3rd)
515 Cannon House Office Building
(202) 225-5406; 225-3103
Erie: (814) 454-8190
Web Site

Rep. Scott Perry (R-4th) **
126 Cannon House Office Building
(202) 225-5836; 226-1000
Gettysburg: (717) 338-1919
Web Site

Rep. Glenn Thompson (R-5th)
124 Cannon House Office Building
(202) 225-5121; 225-5796
Bellefonte: (814) 353-0215
Web Site

Rep. Jim Gerlach (R-6th)
2442 Rayburn House Office Building
(202) 225-4315; 225-8440
Wyomissing: (610) 376-7630
Web Site

Rep. Patrick Meehan (R-7th)
513 Cannon House Office Building
(202) 225-2011; 226-0280
Springfield: (610) 690-7323
Web Site

Rep. Michael Fitzpatrick (R-8th)
1224 Longworth House Office Building
(202) 225-4276; 225-9511
Langhome: (215) 579-8102
Web Site

Rep. Bill Shuster (R-9th)
204 Cannon House Office Building
(202) 225-2431; 225-2486
Chambersburg: (717) 264-8308
Web Site

Pennsylvania cont.

Rep. Thomas Marino (R-10th)
410 Cannon House Office Building
(202) 225-3731; 225-9594
Williamsport: (570) 322-3961
Web Site

Rep. Lou Barletta (R-11th)
115 Cannon House Office Building
(202) 225-6511; 226-6250
Hazelton: (570) 751-0050
Web Site

Rep. Keith Rothfus (R-12th) **
503 Cannon House Office Building
(202) 225-2065; 225-5709
Pittsburgh: (412) 837-1361
Web Site

Rep. Allyson Schwartz (D-13th)
1227 Longworth House Office Building
(202) 225-6111; 226-0611
Philadelphia: (215) 335-3355
Web Site

Rep. Mike Doyle (D-14th)
401 Cannon House Office Building
(202) 225-2135; 225-3084
Penn Hills: (412) 241-6055
Web Site

Rep. Charles Dent (R-15th)
1009 Longworth House Office Building
(202) 225-6411; 226-0778
Bethlehem: (610) 861-9734
Web Site

Rep. Joseph Pitts (R-16th)
420 Cannon House Office Building
(202) 225-2411; 225-2013
Lancaster: (717) 393-0667
Web Site

Rep. Matthew Cartwright (D-17th) **
1419 Longworth House Office Building
(202) 225-5546; 226-0996
Scranton: (570) 341-1050
Web Site

Pennsylvania cont.

Rep. Tim Murphy (R-18th)
322 Cannon House Office Building
(202) 225-2301; 225-1844
Pittsburgh: (412) 344-5583

Puerto Rico

Res. Com. Pedro Pierluisi (D-AL)
1218 Longworth House Office Building
(202) 225-2615; 225-2154
Old San Juan: (787) 723-6333
Web Site

Rhode Island

Rep. David Cicilline (D-1st)
128 Cannon House Office Building
(202) 225-4911; 225-3290
Pawtucket: (401) 729-5600
Web Site

Rep. James Langevin (D-2nd)
109 Cannon House Office Building
(202) 225-2735; 225-5976
Warwick: (401) 732-9400
Web Site

South Carolina

Rep. VACANT (-1st) **
Special Election May 17, 2013
322 Cannon House Office Building
(202) 225-3176; 225-3407
N/A
Web Site

Rep. Joe Wilson (R-2nd)
2229 Rayburn House Office Building
(202) 225-2452; 225-2455
Beaufort: (843) 521-2530
Web Site

Rep. Jeff Duncan (R-3rd)
116 Cannon House Office Building
(202) 225-5301; 225-3216
Anderson: (864) 224-7401

South Carolina cont.

Rep. Trey Gowdy (R-4th)
1237 Longworth House Office Building
(202) 225-6030; 226-1177
Greenville: (864) 241-0175
Web Site

Rep. Mick Mulvaney (R-5th)
1004 Longworth House Office Building
(202) 225-5501; 225-0464
Rock Hill: (803) 327-1114
Web Site

Rep. James Clyburn (D-6th)
2135 Rayburn House Office Building
(202) 225-3315; 225-2313
Columbia: (803) 799-1100
Web Site

Rep. Tom Rice, Jr. (R-7th) **
325 Cannon House Office Building
(202) 225-9895; 225-9690
Myrtle Beach: (843) 445-6459
Web Site

South Dakota

Rep. Kristi Noem (R-AL)
226 Cannon House Office Building
(202) 225-2801; 225-5823
Sioux Falls: (605) 275-2868
Web Site

Tennessee

Rep. Phil Roe (R-1st)
419 Cannon House Office Building
(202) 225-6356; 225-5714
Morristown: (423) 254-1400
Web Site

Rep. John Duncan, Jr. (R-2nd)
2207 Rayburn House Office Building
(202) 225-5435; 225-6440
Knoxville: (423) 523-3772
Web Site

Tennessee cont.

Rep. Chuck Fleischmann (R-3rd)
511 Cannon House Office Building
(202) 225-3271; 225-3494
Chattanooga: (423) 756-2342
Web Site

Rep. Scott DesJarlais (R-4th)
413 Cannon House Office Building
(202) 225-6831; 226-5172
Columbia: (931) 381-9920
Web Site

Rep. Jim Cooper (D-5th)
1536 Longworth House Office Building
(202) 225-4311; 226-1035
Nashville: (615) 736-5295
Web Site

Rep. Diane Black (R-6th)
1531 Longworth House Office Building
(202) 225-4231; 225-6887
Murfreesboro: (615) 896-1986
Web Site

Rep. Marsha Blackburn (R-7th)
217 Cannon House Office Building
(202) 225-2811; 225-3004
Memphis: (901) 382-5811
Web Site

Rep. Stephen Fincher (R-8th)
1118 Longworth House Office Building
(202) 225-4714; 225-1765
Jackson: (731) 423-4848
Web Site

Rep. Steve Cohen (D-9th)
1005 Longworth House Office Building
(202) 225-3265; 225-5663
Memphis: (901) 544-4131
Web Site

Texas

Rep. Louie Gohmert (R-1st)
2440 Rayburn House Office Building
(202) 225-3035; 226-1230
Tyler: (903) 561-6349
Web Site

Rep. Ted Poe (R-2nd)
430 Cannon House Office Building
(202) 225-6565; 225-5547
Beaumont: (877) 218-1997
Web Site

Rep. Sam Johnson (R-3rd)
1211 Longworth House Office Building
(202) 225-4201; 225-1485
Richardson: (972) 470-0892
Web Site

Rep. Ralph Hall (R-4th)
2405 Rayburn House Office Building
(202) 225-6673; 225-3332
Rockwall: (972) 771-9118
Web Site

Rep. Jeb Hensarling (R-5th)
129 Cannon House Office Building
(202) 225-3484; 225-4888
Dallas: (214) 349-9996
Web Site

Rep. Joe Barton (R-6th)
2109 Rayburn House Office Building
(202) 225-2002; 225-3052
Arlington: (817) 543-1000
Web Site

Texas cont.

Rep. John Culberson (R-7th)
2352 Rayburn House Office Building
(202) 225-2571; 225-4381
Houston: (713) 682-8828
Web Site

Rep. Kevin Brady (R-8th)
301 Cannon House Office Building
(202) 225-4901; 225-5524
Conroe: (936) 441-5700
Web Site

Rep. Al Green (D-9th)
2201 Rayburn House Office Building
(202) 225-7508; 225-2947
Houston: (713) 383-9234
Web Site

Rep. Michael McCaul (R-10th)
131 Cannon House Office Building
(202) 225-2401; 225-5955
Austin: (512) 473-2357
Web Site

Rep. Mike Conaway (R-11th)
2430 Rayburn House Office Building
(202) 225-3605; 225-1783
Midland: (432) 687-2390
Web Site

Rep. Kay Granger (R-12th)
320 Cannon House Office Building
(202) 225-5071; 225-5683
Ft. Worth: (817) 338-0909
Web Site

Rep. Mac Thornberry (R-13th)
2209 Rayburn House Office Building
(202) 225-3706; 225-3486
Amarillo: (806) 371-8844
Web Site

Rep. Randy Weber (R-14th) **
510 Cannon House Office Building
(202) 225-2831; 225-0271
Lake Jackson: (979) 285-0231
Web Site

Texas cont.

Rep. Ruben Hinojosa (D-15th)
2262 Rayburn House Office Building
(202) 225-2531; 225-5688
McAllen: (956) 682-5545
Web Site

Rep. Beto O'Rourke (D-16th) **
1721 Longworth House Office Building
(202) 225-4831; 225-2016
El Paso: N/A
Web Site

Rep. Bill Flores (R-17th)
1505 Longworth House Office Building
(202) 225-6105; 225-0350
Waco: (254) 732-0748
Web Site

Rep. Sheila Jackson Lee (D-18th)
2160 Rayburn House Office Building
(202) 225-3816; 225-3317
Houston: (713) 655-0050
Web Site

Rep. Randy Neugebauer (R-19th)
1424 Longworth House Office Building
(202) 225-4005; 225-9615
Lubbock: (806) 763-1611
Web Site

Rep. Joaquin Castro (D-20th) **
212 Cannon House Office Building
(202) 225-3236; 225-1915
San Antonio: (210) 348-8216
Web Site

Rep. Lamar Smith (R-21st)
2409 Rayburn House Office Building
(202) 225-4236; 225-8628
San Antonio: (210) 821-5024
Web Site

Rep. Pete Olson (R-22nd)
312 Cannon House Office Building
(202) 225-5951; 225-5241
Sugar Land: (281) 494-2690
Web Site

Texas cont.

Rep. Pete Gallego (D-23rd) **
431 Cannon House Office Building
(202) 225-4511; 225-2237
N/A
Web Site

Rep. Kenny Marchant (R-24th)
1110 Longworth House Office Building
(202) 225-6605; 225-0074
Irving: (972) 556-0162
Web Site

Rep. Roger Williams (R-25th) **
1122 Longworth House Office Building
(202) 225-9896; 225-9692
Austin: (512) 473-8910
Web Site

Rep. Michael Burgess (R-26th)
2241 Rayburn House Office Building
(202) 225-7772; 225-2919
Lewisville: (972) 434-9700
Web Site

Rep. Blake Farenthold (R-27th)
2110 Rayburn House Office Building
(202) 225-7742; 226-1134
Corpus Christi: (361) 884-2222
Web Site

Rep. Henry Cuellar (D-28th)
2463 Rayburn House Office Building
(202) 225-1640; 225-1641
San Antonio: (210) 271-2851
Web Site

Rep. Gene Green (D-29th)
2470 Rayburn House Office Building
(202) 225-1688; 225-9903
Houston: (281) 999-5879
Web Site

Rep. Eddie Bernice Johnson (D-30th)
2468 Rayburn House Office Building
(202) 225-8885; 226-1477
Dallas: (214) 922-8885
Web Site

Texas cont.

Rep. John Carter (R-31st)
409 Cannon House Office Building
(202) 225-3864; 225-5886
Round Rock: (512) 246-1600
Web Site

Rep. Pete Sessions (R-32nd)
2233 Rayburn House Office Building
(202) 225-2231; 225-5878
Dallas: (972) 392-0505
Web Site

Rep. Marc Veasey (D-33rd) **
414 Cannon House Office Building
(202) 225-9897; 225-9702
Dallas: (214) 741-1387
Web Site

Rep. Filemon Vela, Jr. (D-34th) **
437 Cannon House Office Building
(202) 225-9901; 226-0475
Brownsville: (956) 544-8352
Web Site

Rep. Lloyd Doggett (D-35th)
201 Cannon House Office Building
(202) 225-4865; 225-3073
Austin: (512) 916-5921
Web Site

Rep. Steve Stockman (R-36th) **
326 Casnnon House Office Building
(202) 225-1555; 226-0396
Orange: (409) 883-8028
Web Site

Utah

Rep. Rob Bishop (R-1st)
123 Cannon House Office Building
(202) 225-0453; 225-5857
Ogden: (801) 625-0107
Web Site

Rep. Chris Stewart (R-2nd) **
323 Cannon House Office Building
(202) 225-9730; 225-5629
Salt Lake City: (801) 364-5550
Web Site

Rep. Jason Chaffetz (R-3rd)
1032 Longworth House Office Building
(202) 225-7751; 225-5629
Provo: (801) 851-2500
Web Site

Rep. Jim Matheson (D-4th)
2434 Rayburn House Office Building
(202) 225-3011; 225-5638
South Salt Lake: (801) 486-1236
Web Site

Vermont

Rep. Peter Welch (D-AL)
1404 Longworth House Office Building
(202) 225-4115; 225-6790
Burlington: (888) 605-7270
Web Site

Virgin Islands

Del. Donna Christensen (D-AL)
1510 Longworth House Office Building
(202) 225-1790; 225-5517
St. Thomas: (340) 774-4408
Web Site

Virginia

Rep. Robert Wittman (R-1st)
1317 Longworth House Office Building
(202) 225-4261; 225-4382
Yorktown: (757) 874-6687
Web Site

Rep. Scott Rigell (R-2nd)
327 Cannon House Office Building
(202) 225-4215; 225-4218
Virginia Beach: (757) 687-8290
Web Site

Rep. Bobby Scott (D-3rd)
1201 Longworth House Office Building
(202) 225-8351; 225-8354
Newport News: (757) 380-1000
Web Site

Rep. Randy Forbes (R-4th)
2438 Rayburn House Office Building
(202) 225-6365; 226-1170
Chesapeake: (757) 382-0080
Web Site

Rep. Robert Hurt (R-5th)
1516 Longworth House Office Building
(202) 225-4711; 225-5681
Danville: (434) 791-2596
Web Site

Rep. Bob Goodlatte (R-6th)
2240 Rayburn House Office Building
(202) 225-5431; 225-9681
Roanoke: (540) 857-2672
Web Site

Rep. Eric Cantor (R-7th)
303 Cannon House Office Building
(202) 225-2815; 225-0011
Glen Allen: (804) 747-4073
Web Site

Rep. Jim Moran (D-8th)
2239 Rayburn House Office Building
(202) 225-4376; 225-0017
Alexandria: (703) 971-4700
Web Site

Virginia cont.

Rep. Morgan Griffith (R-9th)
1108 Longworth House Office Building
(202) 225-3861; 225-0442
Abingdon: (276) 525-1405
Web Site

Rep. Frank Wolf (R-10th)
241 Cannon House Office Building
(202) 225-5136; 225-0437
Herndon: (800) 945-9653
Web Site

Rep. Gerry Connolly (D-11th)
424 CannonHouse Office Building
(202) 225-1492; 225-3071
Annandale: (703) 256-3071
Web Site

Washington

Rep. Suzan K. DelBene (D-1st) **
318 Cannon House Office Building
(202) 225-6311; 226-1606
Bothell: (425) 485-0085
Web Site

Rep. Rick Larsen (D-2nd)
108 Cannon House Office Building
(202) 225-2605; 225-4420
Everett: (425) 252-3188
Web Site

Rep. Jaime Herrera Beutler (R-3rd)
1130 Longworth House Office Building
(202) 225-3536; 225-3478
Vancouver: (360) 695-6292
Web Site

Rep. Doc Hastings (R-4th)
1203 Longworth House Office Building
(202) 225-5816; 225-3251
Pasco: (509) 543-9396
Web Site

Washington cont.

Rep. Jaime Herrera Beutler (R-3rd)
1130 Longworth House Office Building
(202) 225-3536; 225-3478
Vancouver: (360) 695-6292
Web Site

Rep. Doc Hastings (R-4th)
1203 Longworth House Office Building
(202) 225-5816; 225-3251
Pasco: (509) 543-9396
Web Site

Rep. Cathy McMorris Rodgers (R-5th)
2421 Rayburn House Office Building
(202) 225-2006; 225-3392
Spokane: (509) 353-2374
Web Site

Rep. Derek Kilmer (D-6th) **
1429 Longworth House Office Building
(202) 225-5916; 593-6551
Bremerton: (360) 373-9725
Web Site

Rep. Jim McDermott (D-7th)
1035 Longworth House Office Building
(202) 225-3106; 225-6197
Seattle: (206) 553-7170
Web Site

Rep. David G. Reichert (R-8th)
1730 Longworth House Office Building
(202) 225-7761; 225-4282
Mercer Island: (206) 275-3438
Web Site

Rep. Adam Smith (D-9th)
2402 Rayburn House Office Building
(202) 225-8901; 225-5893
Tacoma: (253) 593-6600
Web Site

Rep. Denny Heck (D-10th) **
425 Cannon House Office Building
(202) 225-9740; 225-0129
Lacey: (360) 459-8514
Web Site

West Virginia

Rep. David McKinley (R-1st)
313 Cannon House Office Building
(202) 225-4172; 225-7564
Wheeling: (304) 232-3801
Web Site

Rep. Shelley Moore Capito (R-2nd)
2443 Rayburn House Office Building
(202) 225-2711; 225-7856
Charleston: (304) 925-5964
Web Site

Rep. Nick Rahall (D-3rd)
2307 Rayburn House Office Building
(202) 225-3452; 225-9061
Beckley: (304) 252-5000
Web Site

Wisconsin

Rep. Paul Ryan (R-1st)
1233 Longworth House Office Building
(202) 225-3031; 225-3393
Janesville: (608) 752-4050
Web Site

Rep. Mark Pocan (D-2nd) **
313 Cannon House Office Building
(202) 225-2906; 225-6942
Madison: (608) 258-9800
Web Site

Rep. Ron Kind (D-3rd)
1406 Longworth House Office Building
(202) 225-5506; 225-5739
La Crosse: (888) 442-8040
Web Site

Rep. Gwen Moore (D-4th)
2245 Rayburn House Office Building
(202) 225-4572; 225-8135
Milwaukee: (414) 297-1140
Web Site

Wisconsin cont.

Rep. F. James Sensenbrenner (R-5th)
2449 Rayburn House Office Building
(202) 225-5101; 225-3190
Brookfield: (414) 784-1111
Web Site

Rep. Thomas Petri (R-6th)
2462 Rayburn House Office Building
(202) 225-2476; 225-2356
Fond du Lac: (800) 242-4883

Rep. Sean Duffy (R-7th)
1208 Longworth House Office Building
(202) 225-3365; 225-3240
Wausau: (715) 298-9344
Web Site

Rep. Reid Ribble (R-8th)
1513 Longworth House Office Building
(202) 225-5665; 225-5729
Appleton: (920) 380-0061
Web Site

Wyoming

Rep. Cynthia Lummis (R-AL)
113 Cannon House Office Building
(202) 225-2311; 225-3057
Cheyenne: (307) 772-2595
Web Site

U.S. House of Representatives

Committees

Administration
Agriculture
Appropriations
Armed Services
Banking
Budget
Commerce
Education & Workforce
Ethics
International Relations
Joint Economic
Joint Taxation
Judiciary
Reform
Resources
Rules
Science
Small Business
Transportation & Infrastructure
Veterans' Affairs
Ways & Means

Notes : Acknowledgements, Credits, and Sources

All Presidents' quotes retrieved Presidential archives courtesy of U.S. Library of Congress(.gov)

Presidential paper retrieved courtesy of U.S. Library of Congress(.gov) https://www.loc.gov/collections

The Federalist Papers retrieved courtesyzhttps://www.congress.gov/resources/display/content/the+federalist+papers

All supreme court cases, opinions, dissents retrieved courtesy https://www.supremecourt.gov

All scripitual referneces retrieved courtesy NIV Version https://biblegateway.com/versions/new-international-version-niv-bible/

Quotes by Barack Obama - Acting President retrieved courtesy of U.S. Library of Congress(.gov)

Quote Barack Obama - Constitution is "deeply flawed" retrieved www.newsmax.com/+/newsmax/article/326165mobile.wnd.com/2008/10/79225

Quote Barack Obama - "no longer Christian nation" retrieved https://mobile.nytimes.com/2006/06/28/us/politics/2006obamaspeech.html

Barack Hussein Obama retrieved www.conservapedia.com/barack_hussein_obama

Barack Obama quote retrieved "our gay brothers and sisters" https://obamawhitehouse.archives.gov/the-press-office

Barack Obama on religion retrieved www.religionfacts.com/barack-obama

Barack Obama retrieved https://thinkprogress.org

Barack Obama retrieved www.greta-olson.com>docs>jiu_sos

Other quotes Barack Obama retrieved 'Dreams From My Father'

Quote CS Lewis Retrieved www.essentialcslewis.com

Quote GK Chesterton retrieved https://www.chesterton.org/quotataions-of-g-k-chesterton/

N.E.A. retrieved https://en.m.wikipedia.org/wiki/national_education_association

Schools in transition K-12 retrieved neatoday.org/2015/10/08/schools-in-transition-a-guide

www.nea.org/tools/18846.htm

Christian liberties underattack retrieved www.heritage.org

ACLU retrieved https://reason.com/blog/2015/06/29/the-aclu-now-opposes-religious-freedom-b

ACLU retrieved m.washingtontimes.com/news/2015/apr/12/robert.knight-aclu-attacking-pro-life-catholics

Thanksgiving Proclamation U.S. Library of Congress(.gov)

Declaration of Independence retrieved http://www.constitution.org/us_doi.pdf

Constitution of the United States retrieved U.S. Library of Congress(.gov)

Bill of Rights simplified Derived from https://users.csc.calpoly.edu/~jdalbey/Public/Bill_of_Rights.html

Bill of Rights retrieved U.S. Library of Congress(.gov)

List of U.S. Senators retrieved https://www.senate.gov/general/contact_information/senators_cfm.cfm?OrderBy=state&Sort=ASC

List of U.S. Congress retrieved http://www.theorator.com/government/house.html#alabama

All public information, speeches, documents retrieved from the public domain therfore not subject to copyright infringement.